Professional Ethics
for Scottish Solicitors

Professional Ethics for Scottish Solicitors

Alfred Phillips, Solicitor,
Research Fellow of Glasgow University

Edinburgh
Butterworths
1990

United Kingdom	Butterworth & Co (Publishers) Ltd, 88 Kingsway, LONDON WC2B 6AB and 4 Hill Street, EDINBURGH EH2 3JZ
Australia	Butterworths Pty Ltd, SYDNEY, MELBOURNE, BRISBANE, ADELAIDE, PERTH, CANBERRA and HOBART
Canada	Butterworths Canada Ltd, TORONTO and VANCOUVER
Ireland	Butterworth (Ireland) Ltd, DUBLIN
Malaysia	Malayan Law Journal Sdn Bhd, KUALA LUMPUR
New Zealand	Butterworths of New Zealand Ltd, WELLINGTON and AUCKLAND
Puerto Rico	Equity de Puerto Rico, Inc, HATO REY
Singapore	Butterworth & Co (Asia) Pte Ltd, SINGAPORE
USA	Butterworth Legal Publishers, ST PAUL, Minnesota, SEATTLE, Washington, BOSTON, Massachusetts, AUSTIN, Texas and D & S Publishers, CLEARWATER, Florida

A CIP Catalogue record for this book is available from the British Library

ISBN 0 406 12890 1

Typeset by Phoenix Photosetting, Chatham
Printed and bound by Thomson Litho Ltd, East Kilbride

Preface

This book is based on the lectures given by the writer on professional ethics for the second term's work in the Law Diploma course on professional responsibility, during its initial year at Glasgow University. The ideas, which form its structural pillars, took their shape at that time. The reservoir from which it is truly drawn, however, accumulated over more than 40 years' experience as a solicitor in all the main compartments of legal practice, including many of its nooks and crannies. Experience of that sort teaches that, far from making an odd appearance on the occasion of a set-piece ethical dilemma so clearcut as to mimic a textbook problem, questions, qualms and considerations of a veritably ethical nature enter into each and every move made by the solicitor. It is not easy, though, to tap a reservoir of such deep and muddy waters of the professional memory at the right places. But the writer's more than 30 years as writer for, and editor of, first the *Conveyancing Review* and then the *Journal of the Law Society of Scotland* ensured that these murky depths should be continually dragged for whatever was worthy of being brought to the surface. Finally, in the *Lawyer and Society*, published in 1987, the writer set out to explore the place of the legal practitioner within the society in which he functions. This turned out to be an unusual perspective. It led the writer into analyses of, among other things, lawyer's language, lawyer's modes of reasoning and lawyer's ethics. The present book focuses more sharply on the last of these areas and, at the same time, describes how the forces within the lawyer's social environment, identified in the earlier book, have developed and intensified in the intervening period.

Those forces have this year found a political channel, issuing in three Green Papers for England and Wales and a Yellow Paper for Scotland. The Green Papers have been converted into a White Paper, entitled *Legal Services: A Framework for the Future*; the sister White Paper for Scotland followed in October. Perhaps, if one considers its fifteen pages of typescript compared with the other's 105 pages of print, 'daughter' or even 'grandaughter', rather than 'sister' might have better expressed the relationship. An uncanny resemblance in essentials lies just beneath the surface diversity of feature of the two White Papers. Just as the description of the Green and Yellow papers used 'reform' of, implying betterment, instead of 'change' of, so the White Paper for Scotland disingenuously markets itself as 'the Way Forward', suggesting that its provisions represent an *advance*. If the proposals are implemented, no-one can tell what the consequences will be in terms of the restructuring of the two branches of the profession, the reallocation of functions between them, or the relocation and reshaping of solicitors' practices. It is impossible to say, therefore, whether the problem of access to legal services, which is endemic in all societies, will be eased, or be unaffected, or even be made worse by the consequential changes. Lawyers suspect the worst. It is more than a suspicion, though, that the pressure will be on for an all-round drop in the ethical level of the lawyer's professional attitudes and behaviour and for the substitution of lip-service adherence to codes of conduct, which, as the reader will see in the following pages, are incapable of being formulated in any sensible way. What is ultimately at risk is the *culture* of the legal profession, which has steadily evolved over the last century or so and, contrary to the rhetoric of its critics, has shown itself in the post-war period to be adaptable and far from ossified.

The aim of this book is to make that culture express and, in the process, hopefully – as we now say – to help those coming into, and those already in, the profession, through awareness of the cultural environment in which they practise, to stand firm against the feared assault. The lawyer's professional culture is perceived by this writer to be nothing more or less than the ethical dimension of the lawyer's professional responsibility. The Council of the Law Society of Scotland said in its response, published in June 1989, to the Yellow Paper: 'Codification of ethics is not essential for setting the standards of the profession which may be found . . . in the various ethical treatises which are available to solicitors' (although guidance in the form of a so-called Code of Conduct was issued by the Law Society in October). The distinctive feature of this book is its attempt to organise professional ethics in the manner of jurisprudence. That is surely the right form for an *ethical* work.

The writer is most heavily indebted to Professor Alan Paterson of the University of Strathclyde for the food for thought provided by the materials assembled and the problems compiled by him for the Diploma course on Professional Ethics (published by the Diploma Co-ordinating Committee for the Scottish Universities). I have benefited to an unknown, because unknowable, extent from the constant puzzling, in company with the individual partners of my law firm, over the nitty-gritty of professional activity, all of such puzzles having their ethical side. I owe a second debt to my partner, Philip Rodney, for his encouragement when this enterprise might otherwise have flagged. Finally, appreciation for hard work and patience is due to the pilot of our word-processor, Kathleen Cairns.

Alfred Phillips
November 1989

Contents

Chapter 3. Confidentiality   62

Chapter 4. The adversarial system   78

Chapter 5. Standing 108

Chapter 6. Independence   128

Appendices   147

List of cases

Chapter 1

Introduction

Definition of professional ethics

The ethical dimension of the lawyer's professional responsibility encompasses those methods, norms, values and associated concerns which guide the lawyer in the fulfilment of his professional responsibility. Another way of putting it would be that its ambit is the value system of the good lawyer. As such, the area corresponds to what is generally called professional ethics. *The Websters*[1] choose not to define professional ethics with any exactitude, but the organisation of the subject-matter of their book shows that their view of professional ethics is as a collection of duties, to the client, the court and so on[2]. *The International Code of Ethics*[3] is a catalogue of disparate 'rules' ('rules' is their term; for discussion of different usages of 'rules' and related terms see p 136) lacking any defining concept. Close to the conception of professional ethics which we have adopted comes that of the Consultative Committee of the Bars and Law Societies of the European Community (CCBE) *Code of Conduct for Lawyers in the European Community*[4]. Its preamble says:

---

1 *The Websters* is to be taken as a reference to *Professional Ethics and Practice for Scottish Solicitors* (The Law Society, 1984) by R M and Janice H Webster.
2 Deontology is the approach to ethics which focuses on the concept of duty; professional ethics is normally called deontology on the Continent.
3 This refers to the code adopted by the International Bar Association in 1956 with subsequent amendments.
4 This code was unanimously adopted by the twelve national delegations representing the Bars and Law Societies of the European Community in Strasbourg on 28 October 1988; the code represents a development of the principles adopted in the Declaration of Perugia in 1977. The new code was adopted by the CCBE's Deontology Working Party.

1

'Rules of professional conduct are designed, through their willing acceptance by those to whom they apply to ensure the proper performance by the lawyer of a function which is recognised as essential in all civilised societies.'

The point that the 'rules' are *willingly* accepted serves to identify them as ethical in nature, although breach of some rules which goes beyond some degree of gravity may involve disciplinary sanctions. Across the Atlantic, the *Model Code*[5] also recognises the ethical character of professional ethics by grounding its principles within the individual conscience and locating the lawyer's motivation in 'the desire for the respect and confidence of the members of his profession and of the society which he serves'.

Ethics for lawyers not rights for clients

The American Lawyer's Code[6] emphasises its distinctiveness by its approach to lawyers' duties as designed and to be interpreted so as to enhance the basic rights of the citizen (cf. p 10, below: this expresses the American trial lawyers' concept of the lawyer's role). An article by Ruth Adler of the University of Edinburgh, assistant to the Scottish Lay Observer, entitled 'Ten Commandments' ((1988) 33 JLSS 250), is similarly angled but less high-sounding in asking what she postulates to be the key question: 'What ought lay people to expect from solicitors?'. The use of 'ought' instead of 'do' establishes that we are properly in the ethical realm and not confronting a social research topic. But the idea that ethics should be approached from the side of the passive party to the relationship, in this case the layman, although it reflects, in a way naturally, the Lay Observer's legitimate concerns, is, arguably, perverse. The question is flawed in two ways. As we shall see later on, it limits the scope of professional ethics. Perhaps of even more importance is that it ignores the client's

---

5 Model Code of Professional Responsibility of the American Bar Association adopted in 1971, as amended.
6 American Lawyer's Code of Conduct, promulgated by the Commission on Professional Responsibility: revised draft 1982. This was produced out of dissatisfaction with the so-called Kutak Rules designed to displace the Model Code.

inevitably dependent role within the professional relationship, a dependence in relation to not only his lawyer's skills but also his ethics. In neither respect can the client's expectations, or his appreciation of whether such expectations have been realised or not, be enlightened (cf. Perkin *The Origins of Modern English Society 1760 to 1880* (Ark Publications, 1979) pp 253–4). Ruth Adler's question is just the mirror-image of the more apposite but still limiting question, 'how ought the good lawyer to serve his client?'

What is the derivation of professional ethics?

Definition by exclusion helps with the answer. Some argue, on the face of it reasonably, that the *fons et origo* of professional ethics is the law of agency. What is most characteristic of the lawyer's function is that he acts for clients. An alternative designation for a lawyer in former times was law agent, still enshrined in the appellation of the Scottish Law Agents Society. The substance of professional ethics, therefore, can be read off from the law of agency. I would make the directly opposite suggestion that the prescriptions of the law of agency are, themselves, generated from principles of broader generalisation. These principles form part of the structure of professional ethics. In the same way, there is an area of coincidence between professional ethics and the law of evidence in respect of the lawyer's obligation of confidentiality and the evidential protection given to privileged communications between client and lawyer. Again, the basis in principle is the same but the professional duty and the evidential protection are not coterminous. The ordinary law of contract regulates in general terms some aspects of the lawyer-client relationship, but the pattern of mutuality which is peculiar to professional relationships takes a lawyer's obligations far outside the confines of contract. As for the law of delict, its foundation in fault or blameworthy conduct, a grounding shared with ethics, provides a good start for an analysis of lawyer's duties to parties outside the lawyer-client relationship but, as we shall argue later, does not give the whole answer. Our conclusion is that the lawyer in search of professional ethics in general, or for its application to a particular problem confronting him in practice, does not go to his lawbooks. He adopts an ethical approach.

What is the ethical approach?

Stuart Hampshire (in his book, *Morality and Conflict* (Harvard University Press, 1985)) identifies two ways in which a person thinks about ethical issues. In one, he, so to speak, holds up to himself a role-ideal, as a punk or a City corporate adviser or a criminal defence lawyer for instance, in order to shape his character one way or another against that reflected ideal. That approach is unreasoned and intuitive. In contrast to the use of imagination in that way, we sometimes reason out such issues systematically as if from first principles. The source, he says, of those ideals and principles is twofold. Some are believed to be timeless, applicable to all human beings everywhere. To others we feel loyalty as members of the local society from whose conventions and traditions they derive. As regards those former ideals, for example the obligation to respect human life, we would expect unanimity, and instant acceptance of their validity. In the latter case, we are aware that elsewhere and at other times such matters have been differently regarded. In the Kruschev period in the USSR, societies on either side of the Iron Curtain were conceived as continuing to live according to their different values and goals, but in a state of competitive co-existence. Within the same society, we expect broad agreement on first principles and that these should form a reasonably coherent system.

Conflict of principles

Hampshire points out, though, that, as a matter of ordinary experience, reasoning from a single principle does not provide an indisputable solution to a moral problem. Ordinary moral experience, on the contrary, is made up of conflict between incompatible methods, standards, impulses and goals. It is in situations involving such conflicts that moral reasonings and judgments come alive. No resolution can be discovered or upheld which does not involve what Hampshire calls a 'moral cost'. Something of value has been given up or ruled out.

Application to professional ethics

We take the core principle of professional ethics to be that the lawyer should pursue the client's interest. It is safe to say that the basis of the role-ideal, the shared attitude of lawyers in general and the expectations of the society of which the lawyers are members, would all coincide at that point. As we shall see later (p 14 et seq), the application of that apparently simple principle to varieties of situation is not without problems. Virtually each of its terms calls for interpretation, so illuminating ethically grey areas. This writer considers that the other main principles of professional ethics are deducible from the core principle. It already logically involves them, so that together they form a coherent system. Moreover, significant moral conflicts confront the lawyer at points where values and concerns of the local society (in our case, in some contexts Scotland but in most contexts, UK) or those timeless ideals, to which we referred before, compete with the principles of professional ethics.

Example of conflict of principles

Take for example the intertwining principles which may be involved in problems of family law. A high value is universally placed on the protection of the welfare of children; our society regards the married relationship as the favoured matrix for the upbringing of children, but allows the husband and wife a right to terminate the relationship in the event of its breakdown. A solicitor cannot act for two parties whose interests are in conflict, (according to a principle of professional ethics deducible from what we have identified as its core principle; conflict of interest is a main topic in professional ethics; see Chapter 2). If the solicitor is consulted in a situation where a marriage is close to, but conceivably not at the point of, breakdown, he has to decide whether or not and up to what point to mediate, assuming that his professional position makes him influential in the situation. If he holds back from mediation, he may, we would suggest, be culpable from the standpoint of professional ethics. We would regard it as incumbent on a solicitor in certain circumstances to pursue a course directed at a socially valued goal, even in the absence of instructions to follow that course provided that he does so in good faith. (Here we are required to anticipate a later discussion; cf. p 37 *et seq.*) The term 'instructions' is used in a special sense. When we say that the lawyer should pursue the client's interest, we mean his interest as the client perceives it. The taking of instructions is the stage at which the interest, as so defined, is established. If the solicitor persists in mediation beyond a certain point, on the other hand, he may have contravened professional ethics by conducting solicitor-client relationships at the same time with two parties whose interests are in conflict. *A fortiori*, this will be the case where he is truly attempting to preserve the interests of the children of the marriage, since they are third parties from whom he has no instructions. There is a point, therefore, at which his obligation not to act for parties with conflicting interests ought to override other ethical considerations. The determination of that point falls to be arrrived at by a process of reasoning, all facts and circumstances being taken into account. It cannot be pre-ordained by rule.

Do professional ethics set standards or ideals?

The clue to the answer, we think, is to be found at the end of the last paragraph. If the point at which the lawyer's professional obligation (we use 'professional obligation' here as shorthand for the obligation not to act for two parties whose interests are in conflict) should override the other ethical considerations which ought to weigh with the lawyer, if that point were sufficiently determinate to be pre-ordained by rules, then we could properly talk of professional ethics as setting standards. It follows that in our view they do not. What must be said now is that two out of the three model codes for American lawyers make strong claims to do just that, that is set standards. The three are: ABA Model Code of Professional Responsibility (Model Code); ABA Model Rules of Professional

Conduct (Model Rules); American Lawyers Code of Conduct (American Lawyer's Code).

Model Code

In the American codes, qualities are adjected to the pursuit of the client's interest. The lawyer should do it 'zealously' (Model Code) or 'with fidelity' (American Lawyer's Code). Do these words add anything to the core principle or are they just rhetoric, words of encouragement, mere exhortation? They certainly do not lay down a standard, below which the lawyer is deemed to manifest some degree of inadequacy. We may echo Megarry J (as he then was) in *English Exporters (London) Ltd v Eldenwall Ltd* [1973] 1 All ER 727 at 737, when he puzzled over the section of the (English) Landlord and Tenant Act 1954, which stipulated that regard was to be had to the rent payable under the terms of the tenancy in determining a rent under the section: 'How much regard was to be had, and what weight was to be attached to the regard when it had been had?' How much zeal qualifies as zealous?

To be fair, the Model Code puts forward only a very limited claim to be standard-setting. It has a three-way, split-level arrangement made up of canons, ethical considerations and disciplinary rules. In its terms, the canons are 'statements of axiomatic norms, expressing in general terms the standards of professional conduct expected of lawyers'; the ethical considerations, aspirational in character, 'represent the objectives towards which every member of the profession should strive'; and the disciplinary rules 'state the minimum level of conduct below which no lawyer can fall without being subject to disciplinary action'. The full version of Canon 7 says that 'a lawyer should represent a client zealously within the bounds of the law'. 'Norm' and 'standard' as used in the description of the canons are misnomers, according to our – indeed any – definition which seeks to differentiate these expressions from ideals. The low-level, disciplinary rules more or less define the 'bounds of the law' which, according to Canon 7, should set limits on the lawyer's zeal. (For example, DR 7-105 forbids the threatening of criminal prosecution to gain advantage in a civil matter. This would be both criminal and a civil wrong.) It is the middle-level ethical considerations which correspond, in our view, to the proper province of professional ethics. We would criticise the Code's framers, however, for what amounts to a defect in their overarching philosophy, the failure to weld together the discrete groups of ethical considerations into a coherent system.

American Lawyer's Code and Model Rules

The preface to this Code tells us that the ABA have come round to the view that their code is in any event 'old hat' and should be superseded by the Model Rules of the Kutak Commission. The justification for the American Lawyer's Code, its very raison d'être, is its framers' objection to the foisting on American lawyers of the Model Rules. What this Code and the Rules have in common is the position which they both take up on the status of the rules which each promulgates. The Code sets out the substance of professional ethics in the form of an assemblage of rules on the footing that contravention of a rule represents a disciplinary violation. The Code goes so far in this direction as to suggest that its prescriptions represent 'the law of legal ethics'. From our viewpoint, such an assertion is a contradiction in terms. The Model Rules are less categorical in their claims as to status. Indeed, they betray their source in the Model Code by their conflation of the latter's three levels of norms, considerations and disciplinary rules. Apparently, the last of these is the status claimed for the prescriptions of the Model Rules. 'Failure to comply with an obligation or prohibition . . . is a basis for invoking the disciplinary process' (para [5] of note on Scope). But, at the same time, they recognise that ethical problems arise from conflicts which are not capable of resolution by the application of the rules.

Outcome of conflicts pre-ordained by rules

Since the framers of the American Lawyer's Code see themselves as *legislators* of legal ethics, they feel bound to rule on the course of conduct which ought to be followed in situations of conflict of values. For instance, confidentiality, the obligation to preserve a client's confidences (see Chapter 3 on Confidentiality) is generally recognised as perhaps the closest one can come to an absolute principle of professional ethics. Nevertheless, it can readily clash with concerns of our society, which are highly valued, or with universally accepted ideals. So the Code anticipates the potentiality for such conflict by permitting the lawyer to reveal client's confidences where necessary to prevent imminent danger to human life. Within the scheme of such codes, there is no room for consideration of the question whether a lawyer who chose *not* to divulge information obtained in confidence, with the result that human life was lost or great suffering ensued, would be guilty of an ethical breach. A more important flaw in the approach, however, is perhaps that, by legislating for a threat to human life as the *sole* exception of this type to the absolute nature of confidentiality, it stigmatises other considerations of the same sort, such as breach of confidentiality for the sake of the prevention of future or continuing crimes, as disciplinary violations.

Incompatibility between standard-setting rules and ideals

The incompatibility between standard-setting rules and ideals comes out most clearly, though, in the section of the Code designed to maintain professional integrity, synonymous in the Code with what we will call the standing of the profession (see Chapter 5 on Standing). So, for a lawyer to commence sexual relations with a client during the lawyer-client relationship is stated to be a disciplinary violation. Such a proposition can be upheld on the ground that it may represent an abuse of the client's position of dependence within the professional relationship. It is the close proximity in ethical terms to the professional relationship which justifies the status of the prohibition as a disciplinary rule. The contrast is with a lawyer's duty to do a particular amount of uncompensated public interest or *pro bono publico* work, a duty which the framers of the Code say that they endorse. They go on to suggest, indeed, that the imposition of a requirement to do some public work would be justified in the interests of the maintenance of professional integrity. A failure to comply with that requirement would amount to a disciplinary violation. On our view, such a proposal should immediately have been discarded on the ground of its remoteness from that professional relationship. Instead, though, the codifiers suggests that they have rejected the proposal merely because of its vagueness. We would go on to make the point that, apart from its significance as a test of the status of the Code's rules, the lawyer's alleged duty to do some public work has to be scrutinised somewhat coolly and not because it is uncompensated. The reservation comes from the wide scope for clashes between the demands of public work and the lawyer's single-minded pursuit of the interests of his clients (cf. p 19).

Lawyer's role-ideal

Where the American Lawyer's Code deviates from the Model Rules is not so much in the rigour of its standard-setting aspiration as in its conception of the lawyer's role. The Code-framers see lawyers as primarily court lawyers, in the heroic guise of the 'citizens' champions against official tyranny'. Enlisted as champions, their zeal and fidelity in the cause should be unsparing, confined only by far-flung, and for that reason sharply defined, boundaries. In the eyes of the Code-framers, the Kutak Commission, authors of the Model Rules regard lawyers as 'ombudsmen, who serve the system as much as they serve clients'. The Model Rules are, they suggest, compiled by lawyers who write prospectuses for giant corporations.

Fair means

Dershowitz, Professor of Criminal Law at Harvard, sets out his credo thus:

> 'Once I decide to take a case, I have only one agenda! I want to win. I will try, by every fair and legal means, to get my client off . . .'[7].

---

7 *The Best Defense* (Random (NY), 1982), p 47.

Dershowitz certainly sounds like, and definitely is a citizens' champion. (Aside from his professorship, he is a highly sought-after criminal defence lawyer, who led the successful defence of Von Bulow on a charge of attempted murder of his wife, a case notorious in USA.) Yet the admission of 'fair means' into his credo, with its hint of recognition of the requirements of the system as setting parameters for his legal battles, perhaps puts Dershowitz closer to the 'writers of prospectuses' than the Code-framers would imagine. (For a full discussion of the adversarial system as a major factor in the shaping of professional ethics, see Chapter 4 on Adversarial System).

Position in Scotland[8]

Returning to Scotland from the States with its prodigality of codes, we encounter its opposite, frugality. The only areas, relevant for our purposes, regulated by written rules are: retention and accounting for clients' money (Solicitors (Scotland) Accounts Rules 1989), conflict of interest (Solicitors (Scotland) Practice Rules 1986), advertising (Solicitors (Scotland) (Advertising) Practice Rules 1987) and inadequate professional services (Solicitors (Scotland) Act 1988). Those apart, the profession recognises an unwritten system of professional ethics. The situation on the ground in USA, in contrast to the *appearance* of regimentation by the regulatory codes, is described in a letter to *The Times* on 23 February 1989 by an American attorney, (who writes that he is of British origins, with 35 years' experience of law practice in Florida), in these terms: 'The idea that the practice of law is simply a business venture for profit has come to the fore among "trial lawyers" here with disastrous results . . . Ethical prohibitions against lawyer advertising, solicitation, referral fees and cost advancement have been cast aside; lawsuits are bought and sold as commodities'. The purpose of the letter was to criticise the government Green Papers (three for England and Wales,

---

8 This states the position prior to the issue, in October 1989, by the Law Society of Scotland of a Code of Conduct for Scottish Solicitors (see Appendix 7).

the corresponding proposals for Scotland being contained in consultation papers 'The Legal Profession in Scotland' and 'The Practice of the Solicitor Profession in Scotland') published in 1989. His strictures may, of course, be unfair; they come from only one witness. No-one could, we believe, portray the ethical aspects of law practice in Scotland, with its paucity of written rules, in anything like that way. It is this writer's view, however, that regulation where there is already an established system of ethics will have the effect of lowering not raising standards; cf. Chapter 6 *passim*. (In a *Handbook of Professional Conduct for Solicitors* (Butterworths, 1989) by Frances Silverman at p v the field of professional conduct in England is described as a 'maze of rules').

Standards or ideals in Scotland?

We have occasion to comment later on the areas covered by written rules, viz. advertising (p 126), conflict of interest (p 35 *et seq*), inadequate professional services (pp 28–29) but at this point, we can take the Account Rules as exemplary. After all, if there is any field where breach of the rules should be tantamount to a disciplinary violation, it is here. But in an appeal against a Discipline Tribunal decision (*Sharp v Council of the Law Society of Scotland* 1984 SLT 313), Lord President Emslie contradicted the Tribunal's view that a distinction fell to be made between 'common law' charges of professional misconduct on the one hand and on the other hand charges founded on breach of the Accounts Rules or other practice rules, which could be regarded as 'statutory' grounds for misconduct. To the former category , the Tribunal believed, the question whether the conduct was 'disgraceful' or 'dishonourable' was applicable, but in the case of the latter, that is, charges founded on breach of a rule, the Tribunal had thought that somewhat different considerations applied. Lord President Emslie said at p 317:

'There are certain standards of conduct to be expected of competent and reputable solicitors. A departure from these standards which would be regarded by competent and reputable solicitors as serious and reprehensible may properly be categorised as professional misconduct. Whether or not the conduct complained of is a breach of rules or some other actings or omissions the same question falls to be asked and answered and in every case it will be essential to consider the whole circumstances and the degree of culpability which ought properly to be attached to the individual against whom the complaint is made'.

In that judgment, the Lord President expresses at least some of the defining characteristics of an ethical system. Breach of a rule or any other act or omission taken in isolation does not amount to an ethical violation. There are *degrees* of culpability. This opposes the view that a code of ethics provides a handy reference point for strict definitions for professional misconduct (as propounded by Paterson & Bates, *The Legal System of Scotland* (2nd edn, 1986, W Green & Son).

Ethics are a dimension

Our description of professional ethics as the ethical dimension of professional responsibility uses the term 'dimension' with a double significance. The system of professional ethics does, indeed, constitute a *dimension* along with which degrees of blameworthiness can be attached to conduct (as will be seen later, p 58 competence is similarly a 'dimension'). Standards are truly dictated by, and express themselves in, the expectations of 'competent and reputable solicitors'. The role-ideal of the lawyer is a creation of the individual's imagination or intuition. Champion or ombudsman? In no way can the proponents of one view logically persuade those whose intuition leads them the other way.

Chapter 2

Conflict of interest

Extension of core principle

This writer's approach is that the system of professional ethics can be built up from the core principle, as extended to include the social context. The lawyer should pursue his client's interest within the framework of the adversarial legal process against the background of the values and concerns of his immediate community and society, sensitive to those high values and ideals which are believed to apply everywhere and for all time.

Is client's interest always paramount?

If no words at all are added, does the bare statement that the lawyer should pursue his client's interest have no ethical resonance, is it just an excerpt from a job description, as would be the characterisation of a solicitor as a law agent? It is much more significant than that. It suggests the lawyer's identification with the interest of his client. Is it, however, an *identification*, a total immersion in selflessness? If *The Websters'* exhortation to put the client's interest first ('A cardinal principle is that a solicitor should put his client's interest first and not his own') is not to be taken as an alternative expression for 'zeal', their 'cardinal principle', as they put it, should be read literally, that the client's interest should *always* be paramount. It is not a question, then, of identification but of precedence. If self-interest pulls the solicitor one way and his client's interest another, he then has a conflict of interest, which, in terms of the cardinal principle, ought to be resolved in the client's favour? Apart from the possible conflict between self-interest and the client's interest, we shall bring out later the potentia-

14

lity for conflict between pursuit of the client's interest and, in turn, the exigencies of the adversarial system, the values and concerns of the local society and the timeless, abstract ideals. In the face of these conflicts, we shall see that it is *not* always the pursuit of the client's interest which takes precedence.

Hermeneutic approach[1]

Interpretation of the core principle yields these questions:

(a) what difference does it make that the solicitor's real professional life consists of a multiplicity of solicitor-client relationships conducted in parallel and in series?
(b) should the client's interest always prevail over the solicitor's own interest?
(c) what exactly does 'interest' mean?
(d) when does a person become a client?
(e) when does a client cease to be a client?
(f) does 'pursue' imply 'pursue with competence'?

Exploration of these questions will show that virtually all of the key words in what seems superficially to be a plain statement of unexceptionable ethical principle turn out in certain situations to be unclear.

Corporate practitioner

The sole practitioner operating by himself is not the norm. The trend is towards larger and larger groupings of solicitors, with no limit on size discernible at present[2]. Growth has proceeded not only by the assumption of new partners and engagement of new assistants but also by mergers and take-overs. It can probably be said that, whereas growth in size was

1 Hermeneutic is the method of analysis which proceeds by way of interpretation of terms, exploring the full range of meaning.
2 The largest firm in Scotland has 35 partners and 52 assistants, and took on 11 trainees in 1987, 9 trainees in 1988 and 6 trainees in 1989. The largest legal partnership in the world (naturally a firm of US lawyers) has just gone bankrupt.

previously spurred on by the 'big is beautiful' syndrome of the 1970s (economies of scale, wall-to-wall range of services and so on), the stimulant now is the drive to increase market power.

Multiplicity of clients

Only the inhouse lawyer has a sole client. From a professional standpoint, a firm considers itself to have such and such a number of clients; from a commercial standpoint it is engaged on such and such a number of transactions and cases. Specialisation and the factors making for specialisation are beginning to erode the traditional, client-oriented attitudes of solicitors, replacing them with a focus on jobs.

Client-orientation

Client-orientation involves the perception of the client as a person with a problem seeking a legal solution; job-orientation means precisely that, with its implication of anonymity. Solicitors strive to retain client-centred attitudes and ways, despite their corporate structure and the virtual impossibility of keeping up generalistic skills. At the same time, the individual solicitor tends to play down his personal role in favour of an enhanced identity for the firm of which he is a member. Correspondingly, clients are persuaded gradually to switch their allegiance from the individual to the corporate practitioner, particularly where the latter has a charismatic image. The firm adopts a logo and develops a style or personality.

Is ethical responsibility collective?

It follows from what we have said above about the present day structuring of the profession that in nearly all cases (other than the sole practitioner) it is the firm, not the individual lawyer (the advocate, whether a member of the bar or a solicitor, is singled out as the client's sole representative in court proceedings), which pursues the client's interest. Mostly, therefore, it is the firm's conduct which has to be looked at in the first instance in the process of forming an ethical judgment. So confidentiality (the keeping secret of the client's confidences; see Chapter 3), for instance, is to be preserved by the firm and not within the firm. The firm, though, is not a moral agent. Ethical obligations properly attach only to individuals. The second stage, therefore, in the formation of an ethical judgment is to allocate responsibility among the individual partners (perhaps assistant lawyers too) for the firm's breach.

Passing the buck, turning a blind eye

That is not to say that the individual solicitor can easily abrogate his responsibility by total immersion in his deeds and documents, oblivious to what is going on around him. The ethical postures of the three monkeys are not open to him. The same principle applies where a lawyer is working as one of a professional team engaged in a property development or a take-over battle. The lawyer cannot plead that he did not know, or did not see, because he was separated from the unethical act by a chinese wall. In this context, the definition of 'knowledge' in the American Lawyers' Code is apposite:

> 'A lawyer knows certain facts, or acts knowingly or with knowledge of facts, when a person with that lawyer's professional training and experience would be reasonably certain of those facts in view of all the circumstances of which the lawyer is aware. A duty to investigate or inquire is not implied by the use of the words . . .'

Self-interest v client's interest

At one pole, we have solicitors (not only those qualified as such but not practising, but also practitioners) who sit as non-executive, or even executive, or indeed sometimes as managing, directors on company boards. There are also many solicitors who hold high-profile and/or onerous or time-consuming public appointments. Is the pursuit of self-interest with the intensity implied by such commitments, whether or not pursued from self-aggrandising motives or in a manner aimed at self-aggrandisement a breach of principle?

Self-promotion

The CCBE Code (see Appendix 5) deters lawyers from seeking personal publicity for themselves. (The Declaration of Perugia (the 'old Code') imposed a total ban which, in the new Code, has been relaxed to the extent that, in the intervening period there has been relaxation in the member countries. Some lawyers would argue that they do not *seek* publicity, rather it is thrust upon them. The media come to regard them as reliable purveyors of quotable 'sayings of the week' ('the week' usually indicates not just the timing but also the durability of the 'saying') or of instant assessments of weighty events. Most solicitors, though, even desk-bound conveyancers, at some stage in their careers become involved, while in pursuit of their client's interest, in situations which make the news. Depending on personality, the lawyer may be drawn one way or the other: to explain all to the newsman, highlighting his personal role in the process; or to shrink into the dark corner of 'no comment'. If we put to one side the conflict with his obligation of confidentiality, which may well dictate to the lawyer which of those ways to go, it is important to see that to make an ethical judgment in such a situation requires awareness not just of the 'Perugia principle' but also of its justification in terms of the general body of professional ethics. In a society where persons of high standing are also publicity-seeking, high-profile appearances by photo-opportunity-seeking lawyers might work to enhance the profession's standing. Even where that does not apply, the portrayal by the media of a few solicitors in the guise of knights in shining armour would at least do no harm (such an occurrence may be too fanciful; cf. media attitudes in Chapter 5 on Standing). The more powerful consideration which indeed underlies the Perugia principle, is that publicity-seeking suggests the promotion of self-interest over furtherance of the client's interest. People still believe that the true altruist performs his good works inconspicuously.

Non-professional commitments

As we saw (p 10), the framers of the American Lawyer's Code took up the position that lawyers should engage in some unremunerated public service. They held back, however, from the inclusion of a rule to that effect in their 'law of legal ethics' on the sole ground that any formulation of it would be too vague. They regarded such an obligation as designed to maintain the integrity of the profession. The proposition that, apart from the problem of definition, failure to carry out public interest work should represent a breach of a disciplinary rule is, in the writer's view, manifestly absurd. Where such a commitment impinges on professional ethics is surely at the upper limit. The pursuit of the client's interest already contains a strong altruistic element. It should not be pushed into second place by a more diffuse sense of public responsibility.

Outside business interests

The prevailing belief is that there is no *necessary* conflict between the furtherance of such interests and the lawyer's professional obligation. This is accepted to be the case even where a solicitor has substantial, personal property interests and, at the same time, is himself a conveyancer or a member of a firm with a busy conveyancing department. Why should it be necessary even to state that conflict is not inherent in the simultaneous pursuit of personal business *and* professional interests. Is it that the former trespasses on the lawyer's time and attention, which should as a matter of priority be devoted exclusively to his professional interest? More than that, though, personal interests are more exciting, existentially if not intellectually. As we shall see later, it follows from the core principle that in the professional relationship, it is the client who must take the risk. Anecdotal evidence from New York attorneys indicates that, in that commercial hothouse, what they miss most in professional life is the challenge of personal risk-taking. The danger lies in the fact that the more one becomes absorbed in the challenges, the triumphs and the crises, of business life, the paler by contrast appear the client's concerns. Perhaps even, these may be demoted to the point where their primary importance for the lawyer is to provide him with an insight into the commercial world. This argument, it must be said, can be stood on its head. The client may want a lawyer who knows his way about the commercial world, whether that knowledge has been acquired from other clients' or his personal affairs. It should be added that the CCBE Code disfavours participation by lawyers in 'commercial or other activities not connected with the practice of the law' (again, though, the Code recognises that public policy in the member states varies so far as 'forbidden or incompatible occupations' for lawyers are concerned).

Weak version of principle

The more legal practice moves in the direction of specialisation, the more it becomes job-oriented rather than client-centred, the less will a solicitor's personal business, or publicity-seeking, interests be seen as in *necessary* conflict with those of his client. But, needless to say, the adoption of a dual role by a solicitor or too great a concern with self-aggrandisement is likely to be more productive of conflicts between self-interest and client's interest. The weak interpretation of the principle that it is the client's interest which is to to be pursued is that there is no contravention of that principle as long as any such conflict, *when it arises*, is resolved by the subordination of self-interest. It turns out to be impossible to avoid 'double standards'. In the Model Code, these are categorised as 'aspirational' principles and 'disciplinary rules'. Here they are expressed as 'strong' and 'weak' interpretations or versions of principle.

Dedicated lawyers

The strong version is found by a study of solicitors, single-mindedly dedicated to clients' interests, (the vast majority, it is thought), at the opposite pole from those who combine business or public interests with professional interests. Even the dedicated solicitor, though, has more intimate relationships than that with his client, pre-eminently his relationships with his family; and he dwells or has his being (for some hours of the day at least) in a place other than his office. Even then, although in that other place in body, he may still be super-imposing his client's problem on the (for him) disjointed pictures on the television screen. Even asleep, he may arrive at the magical 5 am solution to that very problem, a solution which escapes him, though, on awakening. If the dedicated solicitor yields to family claims, is he in breach of his obligation to put his client's interest first? If he is summoned at midnight to comfort a criminal client newly incarcerated, must he obey even although he knows that his visit can produce nothing of benefit to his client legally? Must the corporate lawyer take the 7.15 am shuttle to London, negotiate points all day and perhaps all night with his counterparts there, and take the 7.15 am shuttle back from London in order to proceed straight to his office to adjust the documentation (perhaps 36 hours non-stop)? There is no regulatory formula, no disciplinary rule, which can provide answers to these questions. One might venture the suggestion, however, that the strong version of the principle is that self-interest in the sense described should be overridden unless the lawyer suffers stress.

Relative standards

Most practitioners will recognise from their own experience conflicts which involve both the 'strong' and 'weak' versions of the principle. Accompanying the conduct which comes out of such conflict will be a sense of something of value having been given up. That is the moral cost (see p 5). The actual outcome of clashes between public or well-publicised activi-ties and devotion to the client's cause, between personal commercial concerns and promotion of a client's business interests (a typical dilemma here would be whether to acquire an attractive investment personally or introduce it to the client), between attendance at a rare artistic performance and finishing off the revisal of a draft commercial lease, between waiting for a wife's first labour pains and dashing to London to represent the client at a crucial meeting[3], will vary from

---

3 It is appreciated that this last example is sexist. It is interesting that in the American Lawyer's Code the exemplary lawyer is sometimes described as 'he' and sometimes as 'she'. Presumably he/she is not undergoing serial sex-changes.

solicitor to solicitor. So will the amount of stress engendered by too many personal/professional conflicts of this sort. So, most importantly, will the judgment which any one solicitor would make on another solicitor's chosen course. That is just another way of saying that standards are relative. It would be appropriate to describe a solicitor who resolved too many of such conflicts in a self-serving way as exhibiting low ethical standards.

Misconduct

At what point does conduct in line with such low ethical standards become misconduct? It is clear that a serious breach of the principle in its weak version would cross the line. An obvious example would be where the lawyer had personally bought a property in which his client had already expressed an interest. A more marginal set of circumstances came up in the Court of Appeal (*Hanson v Lorenz & Jones* (1986) FT Commercial Law Reports 5 November). A client had entered into a joint venture with his solicitors for a property development. In the transactions which eventuated, the solicitors acted for the joint venture. The client's principal claim in court 'was that the solicitors had placed themselves in a position in which their duty to him conflicted with their own interest and that his full, free and informed consent to the transactions was not forthcoming'. The court considered that the solicitors were not under any professional obligations to advise the client as to the business prudence of the venture. The client had to be fully aware of the nature and effect of the transactions before he entered into them and from an objective standpoint the terms must be fair. The propositions that the client is responsible for his own commercial judgments but that he is entitled to look to his solicitors, even though they are also joint venturers with him, for full legal clarification are unsurprising. What is striking is the court's view that the terms, which would also fall, one would think, within the ambit of the client's commercial judgment, should be objectively fair. The rationale lies in the client's position of psychological dependence within the solicitor-client relationship (the court found it in the fiduciary character of the relationship).

Rescue service for stressed solicitors

In cases of stress, a component of any judgment of the lawyer's conduct from an ethical standpoint must be that the lawyer was, or should have been, aware of the conflict between self-interest and client's interest (the significance of awareness of conflict is examined in the context of conflict between the interests of two clients of the same lawyer; cf. p 28). But a symptom of stress, on the contrary, is unawareness that its cause lies in such a conflict. The solution, of course, is to protect the client by referring him elsewhere. (The Law Society has set up a Working Party to recommend how a rescue service for solicitors in difficulties might operate.)

Inexcusable conduct

In a Discipline Tribunal hearing (Decision 367/75(a)), a complaint was laid against a solicitor to the effect that, in relation to a criminal charge against his client, he failed to precognosce witnesses, to arrange a consultation with counsel prior to the trial, to lodge a special defence in time, to cite the defence witnesses and properly to instruct counsel. No explanation was given for the solicitor's complete dereliction of duty. (The decision was taken up with the preliminary question of the relevance of the complaint, on the assumed basis that the factual subject-matter could be proved.) The gravamen of the decision was that, even though the course of conduct in question was neither *dishonourable* nor *improperly motivated*, it could amount to professional misconduct if it was *inexcusable* and so could not help but be judged as *deplorable* by professional colleagues. Even on the assumption, then, (this assumption is made purely for expository purposes; as we have said, no explanation was given for the solicitor's remarkably delinquent behaviour) that stress, which had built up from the incompatible pressures of personal and professional concerns had been at the bottom of the solicitor's default, his conduct could still not be excused. Such a judgment is undoubtedly right from the viewpoint of professional ethics. Given a non-professional relationship, the solicitor's conduct might have been quite differently evaluated. The imperative nature of the obligation not to desert the client is a function of the solicitor-client relationship. The judgment says no more and no less than that the client is entitled to place his dependence on the lawyer.

Conflict of clients' interests

As already pointed out, codified professional ethics consist of an assemblage of rules. A consequence is that potential conflicts of principle tend to be neglected. By contrast, our methodology focuses on such conflicts. Professional ethics, from whichever direction they are approached including codification, must take notice, however, of the situation faced by the lawyer when the interests of two or more of his clients are in conflict.

Competition for time

In a different sense, clients, if not their interests, always conflict, that is in the competition for the lawyer's time. From the job-oriented standpoint, the client's sole legitimate claim on his lawyer's time is for the work actually involved in the job. From this narrow perspective, time for the giving of instructions and the receiving of advice and reports on progress, should be limited to what is necessarily entailed in the carrying out of the work. But the frequency, staging, fullness and manner of reporting entirely depend on the psychology of the particular client. Some clients hang compulsively on every move, their well being dependent on each turn of the wheel. ('Compensationitis' is a medically acknowledged state in which psychosomatic symptoms of an accident refuse to clear up until the compensation claim has been settled; cf. 'Accident neurosis: entity or nonentity' 1972 17 JLSS 89.) Some clients, on the other hand, want to deposit their problem on the lawyer's desk at first consultation and hear no more about it until the outcome. The Green Paper (The Scottish Legal Profession: the way forward) brushes such niceties aside with its requirement for clients to be given '*full* explanations of the issues and to be *fully* informed about progress.' Such *absolute* requirements always end up in minimum or token compliance.

Although the Green Paper's rhetoric is consumer-oriented, that should not be mistaken for client-oriented. Both the logic and the thrust of its proposals are, according to the use of the term in this book, entirely job-centred. A client-oriented philosophy of legal practice means large chunks of additional time (see below) for counselling, discussion of interesting or emotionally charged side-issues, answering (instead of merely repelling) criticism and on the many other activities involved in the sideshow (no inference should be drawn that this 'sideshow' is unimportant) of client management (the intensification of competition brought about by the Green Paper proposals would discourage lawyers from using up time in these ways).

Fees

To deal with the conflict between clients for his time, the lawyer has at hand a brutally simple principle, 'time is money'. Here again, the client-oriented philosophy points one way, towards time-charging, and job-orientation the other way, in the direction of pre-fixed scales and percentages. And again, the Green Paper takes the job-oriented approach. Clients are to be told 'likely fees and costs – both orally and in writing'. It is not long since scale fees for conveyancing were abolished on two entirely reasonable grounds. One was their inflexibility and so their lack of direct relationship to the work actually involved. The other was that lawyers ended up by adopting them whole, instead of treating them as illustrative or maximum charges, which they were intended to be.

Scale charges

Lawyers grumbled at the disappearance of scale charges. They felt that they had been deprived all at the same time of guidemarks for quantification, a sound basis for legitimacy and some reassurance against financially illiterate undercutting by competitors. Scale fees had both allowed and justified the client-oriented approach to charging, characterised by cross-subsidisation of some types by other types of work and the devotion of some time to problems related to the legal process or conveyancing system. Generally speaking, what had prevailed until the abolition of scale fees was a 'swings and roundabouts' attitude as between clients.

Cross-subsidisation

Those attitudes which worked in the clients' or the system's interests survived the abolition of scale and percentage-based charges. (The present tendency in legal practice, it is believed, is for a progressive weakening of such attitudes.) The close solicitor-client relationship, conceptualised in the description 'family lawyer', the basis of which was the handling of property matters for successive generations, led to the practice of nominal, or far below cost, charging of wills, trust settlements, testamentary advice, advice on title destinations and miscellaneous family problems with only incidental legal implications or even none at all. The conveyancer's intellectual interest in, and sense of responsibility for, the perfectibility of the system and his love affair with the draftsman's art created over the last century or so an accurate, flexible and sophis-ticated system of well-defined, protected and freely transfer-able interests in land. Insofar as their efforts were directed at the development, maintenance and repair of the system, most lawyers took the view that these should not be charged out to the individual client. In other words, a client should not be required to pay for the rectification of a bad title, a particularly stylish piece of draftsmanship or a conceded revisal in a con-tentious document. The same sort of reasoning could be stretched to justify below-cost charging on the basis of 'what the carriage will bear'. For example, the upkeep of the integ-rity of the conveyancing system is likely to call for more, and more complex, work in the conveyancing of a low-cost tenement flat than a highly priced suburban villa. Can this approach, though, go so far as to justify uneconomic charging or free representation of a client with a claim against, or caught up in a dispute with, a financially far stronger opponent?

Time-charging

Cross-subsidisation between types of work, and even more so, the differential in rates of charging between one client and another inherent in scale and percentage-based fees are distortions from a purely commercial point of view. Time-charging, by contrast, is attractively straightforward, until you examine it. The highest fees will go to the slowest lawyer. A lawyer's expertise will represent a grave financial handicap. The old *canard* about lawyers comes true – a premium attaches to the length and prolixity of documents. The big corporation which imposes tight deadlines for a complicated contract will be charged low fees. Even more fundamentally, everyone knows from his own introspection that time is a crude measure of *effective* intellectual work, particularly of involvement in problem-solving. This shows up strikingly in calculations of the number of chargeable hours in a 9 to 5 day; that is, if we disregard time spent on 'maintenance', eating, coffee-drinking, on office organisation and 'leisure', including chats to colleagues, the venting of frustrations, recreational breaks and the frittering away of time. And even after that, the category of chargeable hours, in all its apparent austerity, still hides extraneous elements like exchanges of pleasantries with clients, other irrelevancies and, the trickiest issue of all in this connection, counselling (see p 29).

The seven pillars of wisdom

By crude time-costing one can arrive at the cost of running a firm or department per chargeable hour. It is not nearly sensitive enough as a method for feeing up to clients. Feeing-up calls for the application to the crude time-charge of (positive or negative) weighting factors. The Law Society's compilation of the factors in fee charging (see the Table of Fees for Conveyancing and General Business, published by the Law Society of Scotland) are familiarly called the 'Seven Pillars of Wisdom'. (not to be confused with the seven principles, also so designated by the authors, into which professional ethics are distilled in *The Websters*). The seven pillars are:

(a) the importance of the matter to the client;
(b) the amount of any money or the value of any property involved;
(c) the complexity of the matter or the difficulty or novelty of the questions raised;

(d) the skill, labour, specialised knowledge and responsibility involved on the part of the solicitor or assistant;
(e) the time expended;
(f) the length, number and importance of any documents or other papers prepared or perused;
(g) the place where and the circumstances in which the services . . . are rendered, including the degree of expedition required.

At least two of these factors, (c) and (d) are inaccessible to the client. He will be unable to appreciate to a significant extent either the special skill or knowledge required to deal with his problem or transaction or its complexity. In addition, the real value of the basic unit, the chargeable hour, will vary from individual to individual on an intangible scale, and not just in proportion to relative skill. The true variable is diligence, a function of character or concentration plus intellectual quality. For any sort of 'objective' assessment of these crucial factors involved in the fee, the client must rely on the judgment of an insider, a skilled practitioner or a specialist in the feeing-up of solicitors' accounts. (The client can demand that the solicitors' account be checked for fairness and accuracy by the Auditors of Court. The process is called 'taxation'. Taxation of the account is a precondition of a court decree for its recovery from the client.) As with so many other facets of professional responsibility, strikingly exemplified by competence, misconduct, ethical breaches, as we have seen, 'objective' assessment depends almost totally on such insider judgments.

Inadequate professional services

By the Solicitors (Scotland) Act 1988, power was given to the Law Society to direct solicitors to waive or reduce fees and outlays in respect of inadequate professional services. This has been translated into 'shoddy work'. Effectively, this introduces a new, negative weighting. In procedure, though, it is triggered by a client's complaint to the Law Society. It is, therefore, a disciplinary matter. There is a strong argument that the underlying concept is confused. Do you look at the outcome (surely the criterion of 'inadequacy') or the quality (surely the criterion of 'shoddyness') of the work? If the focus is on the latter, is the emphasis to be placed on effectiveness ('adequacy') or just appearance-typographical errors, poor quality notepaper, smudges, and bad sentence construction?

Importance to the client

For objectivity in some factors, then, the client has to rely on professional assessment. In relation to factor (a), though, (the importance of the matter to the client) what is going to count are subjective considerations on the client's side. But there has to be some objectivity here too. Clients are capable of becoming obsessed with what are really minor matters. Some clients are egotistical and feel that anything in which *they* are involved fills the whole universe. The very essence of the lawyer-client relationship, consisting as it does of a monopoly of concentration on the interest of only one of the parties to the relationship, tends to foster egotism in some clients, (but dependence in some and an unpleasant combination or alternation of both of these in others). In compiling the fee, such subjective distortions of the realities must be discounted – rather must not be exploited.

Counselling

Every legal problem, though, has a personal dimension and each unitary solicitor-client relationship has a scale of psychological dependence of the client on the solicitor. There are different levels of demand for information, advice, explanation, answers to criticism, outspoken or veiled – and, above all, for counselling. What counselling, if effective, provides is a compound of psychological support, practical philosophy and moral guidance. So the question becomes, to what extent should the work entailed in the satisfaction of such demands as these, which are the outward manifestation of the matter's importance to the client, be reflected in the fee.

Opportunity cost

The point should be made that the Law Society's seven pillars should be eight, the eighth point being the opportunity cost.

This represents the fee which the solicitor could have earned from another client if he had not lost the opportunity to do so through involvement in the client's work. It is implicit that the lost opportunity would have given rise to a fee substantially higher on the basis of the 'seven pillars' than the fee in question. A more subtle implication is that, in order to justify the charge to the client of the opportunity cost, the client must be regarded as having some awareness of the cost to the lawyer of the lost opportunity. On examination, the opportunity cost factor is just the obverse side of the factor, the importance to the client (factor (a)). Factor (a) is measured by the client's anxiety or sense of urgency so far as communicated to the lawyer. The opportunity cost arises from the lawyer's responsiveness. From the angle of the opportunity cost, therefore, we arrive at the same question as we did in relation to factor (a). If the lawyer yields to what in this context may be appropriately called the client's distorted sense of the realities of his situation and so loses the opportunity of another client's more remunerative work, should the client have to make it up to the lawyer in the fee?

One meaning of professionalism

The answer begins by considering that one meaning of professionalism is that the professional does for money what the amateur does for nothing or for love (for full discussion of this obvious but important point see Chapter 5 at p 121). That comes out starkly, of course, in the feeing situation. It is particularly so in relation to charges which reflect factor (a) or opportunity cost. In cases where the sense of urgency, which is measured by these factors, represents a distortion of reality, we traced that to egocentricity or distress. As for egocentricity, an adviser should urge on the egotist a sense of proportion. And as far as distress is concerned, there is a moral obligation on anyone to relieve it where one can, even at the cost of lost opportunities. Factor (a) and opportunity costing, on the contrary, would make capital out of human weaknesses and commercialise moral obligations. Worse still perhaps, and more generally, the core principle is being stood on its head; not only is the client's interest not being put first, it has instead become adversarial. In this conflict of interest situation, though, the client is not sent away to be represented by another solicitor (see p 55). If aggrieved, the client can request taxation. Aggrieved he may be, but how can he know whether his grievance is justified? Harold Perkin, social historian, writing in 1979 (*The Origins of Modern English Society 1760 to 1880*) said of the legal profession that:

'. . . fees . . . were not in theory fixed by competition, but by the value set by the profession, and accepted by society, on services which the client could not judge and had therefore to take on trust'

Other elements in professionalism

The attitude of trust, which the client is compelled by the nature of things to adopt, corresponds to, better is the counterpart of, that important element in professionalism, the quasi-parental, protective, caring attitude. (References to this element which is distinctive of professionalism recur throughout this book. To avoid repetition, it is encapsulated in the word 'altruism'.) That must come into play in the fixing of the fee. Yet another nuance of professionalism is relevant here, that the professional is entitled to payment only where his trained and qualified expertise has been utilised. Should counselling then not be free, since the solicitor is not a trained or qualified counsellor? Against that, there can be ranged the argument that counselling may be effective, where otherwise it would not, *just* by virtue of the complementary attitudes of protectiveness and trust inherent in the solicitor-client relationship. If the lawyer succeeds, through the moral authority derived from his position, in healing a family rift or facilitating a reconciliation (two examples given in the comment in the Law Society's General Regulations), is he not entitled to a fee? If he fails in his endeavours, is he still so entitled? In the process of counselling, perhaps the lawyer has lost the opportunity to draft a commercial lease or adjust court proceedings. Many lawyers will tell you that 'truly' chargeable hours (time spent on 'proper legal work' like drafting commercial leases or adjusting court proceedings) accumulate only after the switchboard has closed down at 5 pm.

Legal aid

As we have seen, there are many different professional pressures on the lawyer to spend hours of his time uneconomically. Counselling and rectification of flaws in titles are obvious examples. Cross-subsidisation (see p 26) is possible only because some types of work command higher rates of fees than others. Legal-aided work falls decidedly into the category of 'others'. To the extent that a lawyer is commercially oriented, he will avoid or skimp on this category, including legal-aided work. It is accepted within the profession that legal aid does not cover the true costs of proper work. The consequence is that it will be done either by solicitors of high competence out of altruism, or by lawyers of average competence skimpily, or by solicitors of low competence because they do not attract other work. Up to a particular but indefinable point, most lawyers will, in an uncalculating way, do some uneconomic work. Increasing commercial pressures, including that resulting from the government encouragement of competition, means that lawyers now are, indeed require to be, much more calculating in their allocation of time. The spectre of insolvency among solicitors has recently reared its head to the Law Society's concern. This is the most telling indication possible of the trends which we have been discussing.

Other pressure points

There are certain situations where the lawyer's self-interest and the client's interests commercially conflict. One type of situation of that sort is long-standing. It is where the lawyer is negotiating a settlement for his client which includes payment of his client's fees to him by the other side. The lawyer has an obvious commercial interest in an increase in his fee or in the other side's contribution to it, even if that means a corresponding reduction in the settlement figure for his client. The lawyer may yield to such an illicit temptation calculatedly or thoughtlessly. In such a situation, professional ethics demand that the fee element in the settlement is discussed with the client. He remains the paymaster. If an excessive amount is recovered in name of the lawyer's fee the surplus belongs to the client. The reverse situation is commoner. Here, the other party, who is responsible for the lawyer's fee under the agreement with his client, puts a cap on the amount. In that case, the shortfall becomes the client's liability. A similar pressure point is disclosed in the concept of 'best advice' in rulebooks under the Financial Services Act 1986 (for a full discussion of such rulebooks, see p 131 *et seq*). Where a lawyer receives any commission in respect of any service or financial product brought to him on his client's behalf, this falls to be disclosed to the client. Where he does not, he is entitled to a fee for the relevant services. In the comparison of available financial products, 'best advice' may take into account any fee which would otherwise be chargeable by the agent in lieu of a commission. (The conflict between the lawyer's self-interest and the client's interest is at its sharpest in attempts to recover unpaid fees; for discussion of one aspect of this clash, see Chapter 3, p 75.)

Conflict of interest

The most pervasive conflict of interest comes from the fact that the solicitor-client relationship is in practice multiple and so clients compete for the lawyer's time. The lawyer is the professional equivalent of a polygamist with a hundred wives. The lawyer experiences it as an unending struggle. We have just showed also that even the most sensitive exercise of the art of feeing is doomed to fail to reflect with any exactness the relative claim made by each of his clients on the lawyer's time, effort, sympathies and patience. This competition among clients, though, becomes acute in the true conflict of interest situation. Indeed, conflict of interest may be regarded as at the heart of professional ethics (this can be said of confidentiality also; see Chapter 3). A true conflict of interest situation is where the interests of two (or more) clients of the same firm are in conflict. The most vivid example is where one instructs the raising of a court action against the other. It is obvious from the essential definition, that the lawyer pursues his client's interest, that if two such interests are in conflict, the lawyer has a problem. *The Websters* quote a judicial description of this problem: 'It is hard for any man to serve two masters'.

But, as we have just been saying, a solicitor has a multiplicity of clients, he serves many masters. The American Lawyer's Code speaks of 'divided loyalty'. This again misses the point. Loyalty is ethically divisible between two interests as long as the interests are compatible. What it comes down to is that no translation offers as apt a description of the situation where one client's interest pulls the lawyer in one direction and another client's interest draws him the opposite way as the use of the word 'conflict'.

Adversarialism and conflict of interest

We spoke earlier of the framework of the adversarial legal process within which the client's interest fell to be pursued. By that we meant that, not just litigation or negotiation but all legal transactions were adversarial, indeed that all legal process was essentially adversarial. Were we also implying that the interests of the parties confronting each other in all of these situations and transactions were *necessarily* in conflict? The wedding ceremony, which solemnises the marriage contract, although a legal process, is perhaps the purest expression of harmony. But it *appears* non-adversarial only because the terms are standard. When dissension broke out around the inclusion of love, honour and obedience as bridal obligations in the Anglican form of marriage, the adversarial elements in the marriage contract stood out. Lawyers, though, do not attend on, far less pursue the respective interests of, the bride and groom at the wedding ceremony. They may do, in anticipation of the marriage, in the drawing up of an ante-nuptial contract; and they will do if the marriage founders. In either of these situations – the conclusion of the ante-nuptial contract or the breakdown of the marriage – should one solicitor act for both parties? On the contrary, it is accepted that each party should be separately represented. Although these situations share an adversarial character with the wedding ceremony, they call for representation by two solicitors while the marriage requires none. Is that then because they contain a conflict of interest, as distinguished from the marriage, which does not? The logically prior question, however, is, how is a conflict of interest to be recognised.

Conflict of interest rules

The Solicitors (Scotland) Practice Rules 1986 prescribe when a solicitor may not act for two or more parties because of conflict of interest. What follows is a fair summary of the Rules for our purpose (the recognition of conflict of interest), assuming that the solicitor is a sole practitioner (the interpretation of the Rules is more complicated in the case of a firm consisting of two or more solicitors):

(a) solicitor not to act for two or more parties whose interests conflict;

(b) solicitor not to act for seller and purchaser or landlord and tenant of residential property if seller or landlord is a builder or developer;

(c) in certain specified transactions, solicitor may act for both parties, provided that their interests do not conflict, that no dispute arises or might reasonably be expected to arise between the parties and that at least one of the parties (specifically, the purchaser, tenant, assignee or borrower) is an established client;

(d) solicitor may act for both parties in any of the specified transactions if there is no other solicitor in the vicinity whom the client could reasonably be expected to consult. (If the scheme of the Rules is analysed, this is seen to have very limited application; it would apply, for example, where the only solicitor in the vicinity had the seller, lender, etc as an established client. Contrary to perhaps first impressions, the problem of availability does not allow the solicitor to escape from the prohibition against representation of two or more parties whose interests conflict. The Rules are reproduced in full in the Appendix.)

Effect of Rules

The first point of interest to us is the provision that breach '*may*' amount to professional misconduct. In the same context, the US codes use '*shall*'. It follows from what we have said before (cf. p 12, per Lord President Emslie in *Sharp v Council of the Law Society of Scotland* 1984 SLT 313) that the

Rules do no more than give some pointers to an area of professional ethics which is already well understood. Do they illuminate the concept of conflict of interest which underlies them? The prohibition against one solicitor acting for both parties when their interests conflict remains intact. (All of the permissive sections are stated to be without prejudice to that prohibition.) The philosophy of the Rules is that the interests of the parties to the specified transactions, which are all clearly of an adversarial nature, are not to be regarded as *necessarily* conflicting.

Within the range of the specified transactions, the Rules target two situations, defined in general terms but exemplified by:

(a) the situation where the lender is an established client and the borrower is not (unless the terms of the loan have been agreed before the solicitor has obtained instructions from the lender);

(b) the situation where the seller etc is a builder or developer.

The rationale behind these special situations is the acknowledged inequality in bargaining power between the lender, by virtue of his provision of finance, and the borrower and similarly, but for different reasons, between the builder or developer of residential property and the purchaser or tenant. As a result of such inequality, the strong party is in a position to push for leonine terms not only during the negotiations, but throughout the adjustment of the conveyancing documentation, a position against which the weaker party requires independent advice and protection. A conflict of interest is, therefore, more or less inevitable.

Disputes

Apart from that, the Rules do not attempt any definition of conflict of interest, or delineation of the situations in which it arises. To be fair, they do place an explicit embargo on situations where a 'dispute arises or might reasonably be expected to arise'. We can go so far then as to say that a dispute implies a conflict. But we cannot add that the absence of a dispute means that there is no conflict. One solicitor cannot act for the opposed parties in a court action or in a dispute which, if not resolved, could lead to a court action. Could a solicitor act for both parties to a 'friendly', undefended divorce? Here, there is no dispute, the parties are unaware of any conflict. Nonetheless, it is generally accepted that the lawyer should not act for both. (The American Lawyer's Code is liberal on this point. Its stance is that the lawyer can properly act if both parties voluntarily consent.) Why?

Meaning of 'interest'

The client's interest, quite simply, is what the client perceives it to be. That perception will not necessarily – indeed is unlikely to – correspond closely to the client's conception of what his interest is at the time when he first sits down in front of the lawyer's desk. 'Taking instructions' is the process of reaching agreement, or at least a common position, between lawyer and client on what is the interest to be pursued. The process must involve a dialogue. It should, in most cases and at least in part, be dialectical with the lawyer as devil's advocate. The dialogue may well include moral, psychological and financial considerations, as well as forecasts of the possible outcome of alternative courses of action or inaction. Does the client really want to embark on an oppressive, although possibly legally justifiable, course? Does the client have the stamina for an abrasive litigation? What will exacerbation of the dispute do to his commercial or personal relationships with the antagonist? Can he afford the cost?

Client's interest and morality

It is at this stage that the lawyer has his best opportunity to urge on the client such public interest considerations (we use this term here and later for what, following Hampshire, we previously described as the values and concerns of the local society) as the lawyer considers to be germane to the client's situation. He may also as a matter of personal principle attempt to persuade or dissuade the client into or from a course concerning which the lawyer has strong moral views.

This requires great circumspection and sensitivity. In general terms, a lawyer should not try to substitute his values for those of the client. A Roman Catholic lawyer, for example, should not be seen on grounds of conscience to persuade his client not to sue for divorce. Nor should a Thatcherite lawyer advise that a clause of exclusivity should be dropped from an agreement because of its anti-competitive effect (provided always, of course, that the clause is neither unlawful nor unenforceable). On the other side of the coin, a New York law firm withdrew its services from an established client, South African Airways, as a protest against apartheid. That happened before the imposition of sanctions on South Africa by the US. In the recent anti-trust litigation in the New York courts which had the effect of frustrating the take-over bid by Minorco for Goldfields, Minorco had known South African connections. Criticism for the support given to Minorco by American concerns was levelled, it was reported, not at the law firm which represented Minorco but at Chemical Bank which had provided some of its finance.

Hired guns and taxicabs

As a matter of professional ethics, a lawyer is justified in seeing his role as that of a 'hired gun', a more graphic version, perhaps, of the American Lawyer's Code's 'champion against the world' (see p 10). Once he has gone through the process of taking instructions, the lawyer can act for no matter whom in pursuit of that person's interests as that person perceives it, provided that the means and the objective are lawful (as well as unlawful means, unfair means may be ethically proscribed; see Chapter 4, *passim*). The more reputable use of the hired gun is as a bodyguard. But he can also be engaged as a killer. So, although we have said that the lawyer is *justified* in representing persons of disrepute in pursuit of unpopular or even unsavoury objectives, is he bound to do so? Such an obligation, where it exists, is called the cab-rank principle. A lawyer must take whatever fare presents himself to whatever destination, always remaining within the law. Members of the Bar in the UK adhere to the cab-rank principle. Cynics point out that their adherence to it is more theoretical in practice than real. Even if the advocate is supposed to be at the rank, he often turns out to have a prior engagement. More disconcertingly still, he may make the client change taxis *en route* to allow *him* to change fares. The rationale of the cab rank principle is that every citizen is entitled to legal representation. This unexceptionable principle is vulnerable to the radical attack that taxis are not there to give lifts. The taxi will take a rich man to the house of ill-fame but not the poor man to his home.

Ought the solicitor to follow the cab rank rule?

In our view, the profession collectively is under an obligation to provide anyone, who can pay or is funded (see p 26 *et seq* for discussion of the extent of the individual solicitor's obligation to persons who fall into neither category), with representation by a solicitor. The Law Society, on request, will nominate a solicitor to implement that responsibility. The individual solicitor is regarded as free to decline to act on grounds of conscience, principle or repugnance. Such a ground would require to be stronger in the case of an established client, strong enough to override the sense of loyalty. There are two marginal cases. Put in the form of questions, these are: ought the solicitor to turn away a client in the absence of any such ground, for instance, because of social class or because the opportunity cost (see p 29 *et seq*) is too high and is likely to be irrecoverable?; ought the lawyer to avoid the risk of disrepute by association? We will not answer these questions. In particular circumstances, suggestions as to the answer to the first question may lie elsewhere in these pages; consideration of the second question is postponed to Chapter 5. Everyone would admit – although some might retain private reservations – that it is in the public interest that persons accused of at least serious crimes should have legal representation.

Withdrawal by lawyers on grounds of conscience etc

What emerged during our analysis of the meaning to be given to 'interest' was the possibility of conflict, not between the interests of two clients of the same lawyer, nor between the lawyer's self-interest and that of his client, but between the client's interest (as the client perceives it) and, ranged on the other side, the lawyer's personal values, the public interest, or abstract ideals (for truth as a value in relation to professional ethics, see *post*). If the lawyer comes to the conclusion that the conflict is best resolved by his declining to act for the client, he should do that sooner rather than later. If, on the other hand, he elects to carry on, despite his reservations, what he must pursue is the interest according to the client's perception of it. Assuming that the conflict is suppressed only to re-emerge in a sharper form or if it appears for the first time at a later stage, a countervailing factor against withdrawal at that stage by the lawyer will be the possible detriment to the client's interest. Rejection at the outset of a piece of business may be easily glossed over by the client (although solicitors' folklore has it that a client moving from one solicitor to another is 'bad news' for the second one). Withdrawal in midstream, particularly during a court action, is apt to be taken as a mark of a weak or dishonest case. On the other hand, withdrawal, far from being detrimental, may be advantageous where dilatory tactics have been adopted. More time will be gained through the opportunity given to the party by the court to find a new solicitor to substitute for the one who has withdrawn. The solicitor should not withdraw for the sole purpose of enabling his client to gain such an advantage.

Effect of consent

Having established the meaning of 'interest' we can return to the topic of conflict of interests in its generally understood sense of a conflict between the interests of two clients of the same solicitor. If the situation is explained to both clients, who want the solicitor to continue to act for them both despite the conflict, should the lawyer agree? Under the American Lawyer's Code, a lawyer may do so if both clients are fully informed of the potentially adverse implications and voluntarily consent. Certainly, it should be so, on the principle that it is the clients' perception of their interests which matters (once the process of giving instructions has taken place). Conflict of interest problems are often trammelled by confidentiality. This is an actual case. A solicitor offers to purchase a property for client A and the offer is turned down on the ground that the price is too low. A stranger, B, telephones the solicitor some two weeks later to say that he has reached an agreement to purchase the same property at a figure which he mentions and which turns out to be the same as the price offered by client A (and previously rejected). He tells the solicitor that he has been recommended to him by another client. B wants the solicitor to conclude missives on his behalf. The solicitor must assume that A's interest in the property is still alive, notwithstanding the rejection of his offer. He cannot *ask* A since the information that the property is available at the rejected figure is confidential to B. There being an irreconcilable conflict of interest between A and B, the solicitor cannot act. To return to the general question, in this writer's view, the position on the effect of consent is not quite so cut-and-dried as the American Lawyer's Code suggests.

Some instances

Mediation

Mediation is the attempt, when a dispute has arisen, to determine whether there is a real conflict of interest. The existence of a dispute means that the parties perceived their interests as being in conflict. Mediation consists of the same sort of exploration of the clients' interests as in the process of taking instructions. If at the end of the process the parties remain in dispute, then the effort at mediation has failed and a conflict of interest situation exists. Mediation of disputes is in the public interest, but the role of mediator is a dangerous one for the solicitor to play. Once embarked on the process, the lawyer is not truly wedded to either client's interest. Nor is mediation a case where the public interest consideration should have any force alongside the clients' interests. The alternative to mediation is to refer to another solicitor one of the clients in dispute. To part with the client has the serious drawbacks which we mention below (p 55). In addition, at least initially, its effect is to sharpen the dispute by widening the psychological gap between the parties.

Negotiation

Rule 5 of the Solicitors (Scotland) Practice Rules 1986 forbids a single solicitor to act in the specified transactions – sale and purchase of heritable property and so on – even in the exceptional cases which it delimits, if a dispute has arisen. The Rule, reasonably enough, does not envisage any scope for mediation in these purely commercial transactions. For the purposes of the Rules, a transaction is taken to run from the pre-contract stage right through to completion. The wrong impression may be gathered that the solicitor can enjoy the same freedom to represent both parties in the adjustment of the contractual terms as with the terms of the conveyance. The Rules, however, do not in the least subtract from, indeed they entrench, the prohibition against acting for both parties when their interests conflict. Negotiation is the process by which the contractual terms are adjusted. Negotiation, properly defined, is an interchange between parties whose interests conflict. We consider it axiomatic, therefore, that the same lawyer cannot act for both sides to a negotiation.

Transactions

Once negotiation has issued in agreement on the contractual terms, the solicitor can act for both parties to the transaction, according to the Rules, unless a 'dispute arises or might reasonably be expected to arise between the parties'. (For our present purposes, it is appropriate to put to one side the other qualifications in the Rules.) In this writer's view, the presence or reasonable expectations of a *dispute* is not the right criterion. Whether or not a dispute arises depends on the response to an existing or emergent situation by the client. The conflict of interest precedes any such dispute. As we have seen, a conflict may not give rise to a dispute and there may be a dispute without a conflict. The determinant is whether there is an emergent conflict. Transactions, being adversarial, contain the seeds of potential conflict of interest. This immediately prompts the question: how, in the absence of supervening circumstances, can there be a potential conflict without there being a present conflict? The answer lies in the lawyer's educated expectations, educated, that is, by training and experience he is able to form a reasonable expectation as to whether at some stage he will feel himself bound to advise one client that his interest lies one way and the other client that *his* interest is opposed. The conflict is potential only in that sense.

Commercial lease and residential lease compared

It would be an act of extreme professional irresponsibility for one solicitor to act for both landlord and tenant in a commercial lease. That can be said even though it is normal for such a transaction to come to the lawyer at the stage where the main terms, rent, duration, review frequency and so on, have already been agreed. The seasoned commercial conveyancer is well aware that potential conflict between the landlord's and the tenant's interests inhere in every other provision of the lease. The lawyer should resist the strongest blandishments from his clients to act for both. Many solicitors, though, would act for both parties to a residential lease. The difference is that, once the rent etc have been agreed, the rest of the terms are regarded as standard. The lawyer's reasonable expectation is that he will not be placed in the invidious position which would almost certainly confront the conveyancer of the commercial lease. There can be said to be no conflict of interest. The prudent lawyer, though, will want to check his reasonable expectations with the prospective tenant before he agrees to act for him, for the residential lease is undoubtedly adversarial in nature. For example, insofar as any species of repair is included within the tenant's liability the landlord is relieved of his obligation. To the extent that the landlord is entitled to recover possession, the tenant does not have security of tenure. If the tenant confirms that his perception of his interest coincides with the standard terms, the ethical solicitor can act for both.

Non-adversarial interests

Clients may be linked in other ways than as the parties on opposite sides of an adversarial transaction: as victims of a common accident or disaster; as co-accused; as partners where, in addition to the individual partners, the partnership itself is a client; as having one of the complex of interests inherent in an abstract entity with full legal personality, typically a limited liability company; as indemnifier and indemnified; as family relatives. The characteristics of such non-adversarial interests are that they both coincide *and* have a potential for conflict. Insofar as they are coincident, single and therefore single-minded pursuit is not only permissible, but also desirable for uniformity of approach and to save expense. But the lawyer must remain alert to the emergence of conflict. Here potential conflict means something different from what we said it meant in the context of a transaction. If conflict emerges it will be the consequence of supervening circumstances. For example, an ethical lawyer will not act for all the victims of an accident if any of them appears to be to blame to any extent. New facts may emerge which suggest, or the defender's stance may point to, the possibility that one of the victims was a contributory. A conflict has then arisen, the potentiality for which was not previously evident. The solicitor is at fault only if he fails to recognise and react to the conflict situation when it emerges.

Interest of accused

In criminal defence, the lawyer's obligation to pursue his client's interest remains the linchpin of the relationship. What that boils down to in most instances is, in terms of Dershowitz's agenda (see p 10), 'by every fair and legal means, to get [the] client off'. More realistically, most of the time, the objective is more modestly stated as that of ensuring that the minimum amount of blame for the crime should be pinned on a client. This is true of most, but not of all, cases. Exceptionally, the client may want to shield another person to whom he is intimately related. So he may insist that his defence is conducted without implicating that other person. An example is where the client has been accused of tax evasion and the lawyer can see that the fraud has actually been committed by the client's wife, who has not been charged. This example appears in the American Lawyer's Code of Conduct. The

Code, in its best authoritarian manner, pronounces that the lawyer would commit a disciplinary violation if he flouted these instructions. On the principle that it is the client's perception of his interest which eventually counts, that seems to be the ethically justified course. Against it are ranged the lawyer's self-interest in winning the case and the public interest in a truth-based system of justice, particularly criminal justice. The lawyer, in the process of taking instructions, may press on the client these countervailing considerations – at least the latter – in support of the client's obvious self-interest in an acquittal. Nevertheless, in the ethical balancing act, it seems right for the lawyer to accept that the client's wish to protect his wife is entitled to prevail in such a conflict of values. What, though, if the client's self-sacrificial intent is based not on protectiveness towards the other but on intimidation by the other. The answer then is different. The lawyer's instructions are being given, that is the client's perception of his interest is being arrived at, under duress. The lawyer must champion his client even, perhaps first, against those who seek to subjugate him. There are subtler shades of ethical grey between a distortion of an accused client's perception of self-interest arising from a close bond on the one hand and one induced by intimidation on the other. Clients may opt for a plea of guilty, where it is unfounded, to avoid the ordeal, waste of time, or expense, of a trial. They may spurn a defence of insanity on the occasion of the commission of the offence on the calculation that a spell in prison is preferable to committal to a criminal mental institution. There are no codified solutions for the lawyer faced with dilemmas of that sort. As the judges wisely do in similar situations in the legal realm, the lawyer must look at all the relevant facts and circumstances.

Co-accused

The last paragraph involved us in a detour from the main topic of conflict of interest between two clients of the same lawyer. In the present context, we have in mind two or more persons accused of the same or related crimes. We have gained the advantage, however, of seeing that in this domain, the objective to be pursued is not always to be conclusively determined by the client's perception. Our stance is that the lawyer must not find himself in the position where he cannot pursue the interest of one client without, *ipso facto*, harming the interest of another. This translates into the principle that a lawyer should not act for two clients in a matter where a conflict of interest between them is reasonably foreseeable. Here, we believe the American Lawyer's Code to be wrong (see p 40 on the effect of consent) and the Rules to be right in their assertion of the absolute nature of the conflict of interest prohibition. Where there is reasonable foreseeability of such a conflict, the lawyer should not seek client's consent to his joint agency. With co-accused 'reasonably foreseeable' does not equal 'readily foreseeable'. The trial of co-accused may represent an attempt by the prosecution to find the culprit from among them or to allocate among them degrees of culpability. In the emotionally charged swirls and eddies of the criminal trial, the lawyer's efforts to exculpate one of his clients might, unforeseeably, have the effect of incriminating a co-accused, whom he also represents.

Corporate entities

A corporation, such as a limited liability company, represents a minefield for the ethically sensitive solicitor. A company is an artificial legal person, whose embodiment is generally taken to be its board of directors. The board, in turn, for all practical purposes may have its representation in the dominant person of its chairman or chief executive. Thus, the chairman may be the voice of the board which itself occupies a fiduciary position in relation to the company. From the proprietorial point of view, the company is normally to be equated with the collectivity of its shareholders, but sometimes with only a controlling majority of them. The board is regarded as having fiduciary obligations not only towards the company but also towards its employees. Finally, if the company is verging on insolvency, its undertaking is regarded in law as being held in trust for its creditors. The inevitable consequence of the co-existence of these crisscrossing interests within the corporate entity is that the company lawyer is forever fated to skate on thin ice, with seldom any indication on the surface of the possible conflicts of interest which may be occurring below. The problem normally canvassed as a product of this situation is where the company lawyer learns from an official of the company that the latter has engaged in illegal conduct, either against or on behalf of the company (raised in the American Lawyer's Code of Conduct). This can best be looked at in the context of the company lawyer's obligation of confidentiality (see p 65).

Conflict of interest within the corporate entity. The very notion of an artificial entity at one pole of the lawyer-client relationship is at the root of what is perhaps a more fundamental problem. First of all, we might take, as a dreadful warning to the new solicitor, the situation where he is instructed by a real person to act on behalf of a company yet to be formed. If he proceeds, in accordance with these instructions, to enter into a contract on behalf of the non-entity, he has literally no client. It is trite law that, in these circumstances, the lawyer assumes liability personally, not as agent, to the other contracting party. He may, of course, be able to exercise a right of relief, for what that is worth, against the real person who instructed him. Where the company does exist, the instructing voice or hand will still be of a real person, here a company official not its promoter. If the lawyer contracts on the faith of his instructions, he will be able to rely on the doctrine of ostensible authority or a board minute to establish his capacity as an agent. That is law, however, not ethics. How can the lawyer be sure that in every case he is implementing his professional responsibility from an ethical standpoint, that is, pursuing the client's interest as the client perceives it, when the client is an artificial person? The ready answer is that it is the board's perception which must be taken instead. This is no truer than that it is the lawyer's perception which is definitive of the client's interest. Both the board and the lawyer stand in a fiduciary relationship to the company.

Divergence of interest between board and company. The possibility of divergence between the board's interest or the board's perception of the company's interest, on the one hand, and the company's true interest, on the other, emerges clearly in a recent Court of Appeal case (*Byng v London Life Association* [1989] 1 All ER 561). London Life had convened an EGM to put through a merger with Australia Mutual Provident. A substantial group of London Life members was opposed to the merger. The EGM was called for a fixed time on a specified date at the Barbican Centre, London, where several rooms had been booked, connected by audio-visual link. Concerned that the arrangements might prove inadequate, the board had also booked a larger room at the Cafe Royal for the afternoon. On the day, the audio-visual link was defective. When the meeting opened, some members, not yet having passed through the registration process, were still trying to gain access to the meeting. It was clear that no business could be transacted and that the meeting would have to be adjourned, leaving three options. One was to convene a new meeting on 21 days' notice; another was to adjourn the meeting for a sufficient period to allow proxies to be lodged; and a third was to adjourn the meeting until the afternoon when it would be resumed at the alternative accommodation booked at the Cafe Royal. Following counsel's advice, the chairman chose the last of the options, overriding objections from some members present that they would be unable to attend at the Cafe Royal in the afternoon.

At the adjourned meeting, the resolution necessary for the merger was passed. On a challenge in court by a dissenting member, the Court of Appeal, reversing the judge of first instance, declared the resolution invalid, even though the chairman's decision was taken in good faith and was within his powers.

The gravamen of the court's decision was that the chairman had failed to take into account all the relevant factors, particularly two factors of central importance: one, that there was no overriding need to adhere to the timetable for the merger (so that the option to convene a new meeting on notice was feasible); the other that those who could not attend the adjourned meeting at the Cafe Royal would be unable to speak and even to vote by proxy. This is a landmark decision for English law. The court applied the principles derived from *Associated Provincial Picture Houses v Wednesbury Corporation* [1948] 1 KB 223, familiarly known as the *Wednesbury Principles*, developed and hitherto employed as the basis for judicial review of decisions taken in the performance of a public duty, innovatively to the exercise of the decision-making function of the chairman of a board of directors. It is not safe to assume that a Scottish court would reach the same conclusion. Our interest here, however, is to draw on the legal principles to exemplify our ethical analysis.

From our perspective, the court in *Byng* was saying that the chairman's perception of the company's interest was defective. What he had neglected to take cognisance of was that the company's interest lay in the provision of an opportunity to speak and vote for all those members who presented themselves at the Barbican Centre in time and with the requisite qualifications. That overrode such important factors as that the chairman had acted within his authority, in good faith, within a limited time-scale and on counsel's advice.

Now take a case nearer home – home, that is, being the sphere of professional responsibility instead of chairman's duties. Shareholders had required a company to convene an AGM at which they proposed a resolution for the removal of the chairman of the company, who dominated the board consisting of himself and two other directors. The resolution was passed by a majority vote. The effect was to deprive the board of a quorum in terms of the company's articles, which went on to confer a power of co-option on the remaining directors, while allowing them to exercise a caretaker function pending the exercise of that power. What the directors actually did at the EGM was, after a brief pause, to co-opt back onto the board the chairman who had just been deposed. In doing so, they admittedly, acted within their powers and, arguably, in good faith. Applying the *Wednesbury* principles, though, there would be a powerful argument that they had neglected a crucial option, namely to take time to seek out other directors acceptable to the majority shareholders. From a high, some might say unrealistically high, ethical vantage point, one might ask a question of the company lawyers. Was the directors' decision to proceed as they did truly taken in the interest of the company, as a hypothetical individual, standing in the company's shoes, might have perceived it?

Victims of common disaster

Even though procedure for class actions (court action by an individual representative of a class of persons, all of whom have identically grounded claims against the same alleged wrong-doer) does not as yet exist in the UK courts (although it does in the USA), it is common enough for one lawyer to act for all or a group of victims of a common disaster. That has the obvious advantages of savings in cost, uniformity of approach and concerted action. In the *Piper Alpha* case, solicitors acting for groups of the victims appointed a committee to achieve at least some of these benefits. There seems little potentiality for conflict of interest among the clients. But even in the case of such a close concordance of interest, the defender can create a problem of conflict by a proposal to set aside a 'pot' representing the total damages to be shared among the claimants. The same tensions can arise from the offer of a marginally attractive settlement, which some want to accept and others reject. Such a problem was produced for the sufferers from side-effects of Opren, the arthritis-relieving drug, in relation to the maker's, Eli Lilly's, settlement proposals. Where a lawyer was acting for both an acceptor and a rejector, the conflict crystallised in the issue of confidentiality and so will figure in a later discussion (see Chapter 3).

Non-coterminous interests

The court has held in England (in *Huxford v Stoy Hayward & Co* (1989) Times, 11 January) that it was impossible for an adviser simultaneously to owe a duty of care to two parties whose interests were not substantially coterminous. This is similar to the ground on which lawyers argue that the building society's solicitor should not act also for the purchaser/borrower. The same argument would apply with even greater force to solicitors employed by authorised practitioners if the Green Paper proposal for one-stop conveyancing came to be implemented. The converse situation, however, where the purchaser/borrower's solicitor also acts for the building society is commonplace. How can that be justified from the viewpoint of professional ethics when the former is not? The immediate answer which can be hazarded is that the English judge painted with an unjustifiably broad brush. The building society's interest has to be such that it is wholly subsumed within the purchaser/borrower's interest. That latter interest, however, will extend beyond it. To be specific, both the building society and the purchaser/borrower have the common interest that the latter should obtain a valid and marketable title. Without that, the lender cannot acquire a good security. The purchaser's interest goes beyond that to questions of destination of the title, obligations for upkeep, planning considerations affecting amenity, questions of succession and financial planning (those factors which affect value and, therefore, are theoretically of concern to the building society will almost always in practice be relevant only to the purchaser's 'equity', that is, the difference between the purchase price and the amount of the loan).

One-stop conveyancing

In olden times (this is an ironic observation on the pace of change, not to be taken literally) there used to be one-stop conveyancing and perhaps in some places there still is. The single stop was at the solicitor's. He filled in the application form and sent it to the building society. He explained the loan terms to the client and let him know of any problems arising from the survey. Negotiations on behalf of the seller and purchaser took place between their respective solicitors, strictly at arm's length. The purchaser/borrower's solicitor was then instructed to act also for the building society. Here a problem has to be faced which the keen-eyed will have noted as having been skipped over in the preceding paragraph. Is there not a conflict of interest between lender and borrower in relation to the security? One answer is that the consent of both parties is implied, or can be expressly taken, to the joint agency or alternatively that the scope of the agency on the building society's behalf is limited by standard arrangements. Perhaps not legally, but ethically, these alternatives could be regarded as equivalent. But neither chimes with the author's ethical theory that it is the lawyer, not the client, who carries the responsibility for the judgment whether there is conflict of interest or such potentiality for conflict that he should not accept or continue with the joint agency (cf. p 40 *et seq*). What I would say is that the transaction between lender and borrower is adversarial in character. The terms of the building society documentation are standard, once the principal matters such as repayment terms and interest are agreed. The potentiality for conflict has already, therefore, been removed.

Position under 1986 Rules

This corresponds to the terms of the exception under Rule 5(f) to the prohibition against joint agency on behalf of lender and borrower. One-stop conveyancing where the lender's solicitor acted also for the borrower was, it was argued (see p 36), one of the situations against which the Rules were targeted. But where the Rules go awry, in the author's view, is by admitting that very situation back in under Rule 5(d), which provides a dispensation where 'both parties are established clients'. No doubt the framers of the Rules can argue that there exists always the safety-net of Rule 3 with its general prohibition of joint agency in conflict of interest situations. That is yet one more justification of our position that, in ethical matters, codification makes for looser, not tighter, standards (cf. Chapter 6).

Established clients

An established client is defined in the Rules as one for whom the lawyer has acted on at least one previous occasion. In terms of this definition, most building societies are 'established clients' of most solicitors. In this author's view, the difference between an established client and any other client is more ethically significant in the resolution of a conflict of interest situation than in the context in which it is used in the Rules.

Assume that the purchaser/borrower consults the solicitor after completion of the transaction on a matter where the building society has a conflicting interest. For example, the house market has declined so that the value of the property on which the building society is secured is substantially less than the amount outstanding on the loan. The client seeks the lawyer's advice on whether he can just leave town and abandon the property. The building society's interest would be far better satisfied if he stayed on, sold the property himself and made up any shortfall from his own resources. Should the solicitor be influenced in his advice by the fact that he acted for the building society in the constitution of the security? In the author's view, the building society, no matter whether it is an 'established client' or not, is not a person whose interest falls to be pursued in this situation.

A solicitor, say, has an insurance company as an established client. It asks the solicitor to represent one of its insureds in the defence of a personal injury action. In the process, the solicitor learns something which would be detrimental to the insured's claim under his policy with the insurance company (this scenario is commented on in the American Lawyer's Code). Does the lawyer's established relationship with the insurance company affect him in any way in such a situation? Again, as with the problem in the preceding paragraph, the answer flows from the principle that it is only the insured's interest which the solicitor must pursue.

We ought to return now to the dilemma of the company lawyer who learned from an official of the company that he has engaged in illegal conduct, either against or on behalf of the company (see p 47). The company is the lawyer's established client, the official in his individual capacity is not. Here, in our view, the lawyer must regard the individual as the company's representative. He must act on the basis that the company, not the individual official, is the client whose interest falls to be pursued.

Presumptive clients

Rules 6 and 7 describe circumstances where a solicitor prepares a legal document for execution by a person who has not consulted him. An instance is where an offer is sent to one or more prospective purchaser(s), to be executed and resubmitted to the solicitor, who has adopted that course because he acts for the seller (Rule 6). A variant is where a solicitor acting for, say, a landlord provides him with a lease in anticipation of its execution by the prospective tenant. In both sets of circumstances, these acts of the solicitor are deemed by the Rules to establish a solicitor-client relationship with the prospective signatory of the document, so imposing professional responsibility on the solicitor for a person whom he has never seen. The same conflict principles will apply between the interest of the lawyer's original client and his presumptive client (Rule 7, but here the lawyer's professional responsibility is limited, part of his duty being to advise the prospective signatory to seek independent legal advice before signature).

Vicarious clients

There are recognisable cases, analogous to those figured in the Rules, where the lawyer's client may be dubbed vicarious rather than presumptive. These are cases where a 'friend' acts as an intermediary between the lawyer and the 'client', who may or may not be hypothetical and may or may not have a concealed conflict of interest with the intermediary. Lawyers learn to be chary of such triangular relationships, less so at the dinner-party, where what is sought is no more than interesting conversational gambit, but much more so at the (now proverbially suspect) free lunch. It is not unknown for the lawyer later to find himself on behalf of an established client on the opposite side of an adversarial transaction from the supposed intermediary. Pragmatically speaking, a lawyer should not allow himself to engage in shadow-play. Lawyers must beware of the vicarious client and of the intermediary, particularly if he is himself a professional. The bank manager who wants a 'simple will' drawn up for his customer to sign is a typical example. Such an arrangement is, of course, taboo for the lawyer in terms of the fundamental principle that the interest to be pursued is determined after instructions have been taken from the *client*. A critical part of this process of taking instructions, as we have seen, is the dialogue with the lawyer. Practitioners in a departmentalised firm are well aware that it is unsatisfactory for instructions in relation to a dispute which may lead to litigation to be taken by a partner or colleague in, for example, the conveyancing department. This is an argument which should be put in opposition to the proposal for multi-disciplinary practices to counter the naive conception of one-stop services. True, the different services are juxtaposed. The resulting problem of confidentiality creates the need for chinese walls. But the administrative 'distance' between the providers of the services may well rule out any advantage gained from the physical juxtaposition.

Conflict of interest myopia

The Websters suggest that a solicitor may have difficulty in spotting when a conflict of interest has arisen. We have demonstrated the still greater difficulty of determining the potentiality for conflict of interest, involving as it does its reasonable foreseeability (cf. p 42 *et seq*). Does myopia or resistance lie at the bottom of these difficulties? It is obligatory for the lawyer faced with an actual or potential conflict of interest between two clients to refer at least one. If the lawyer foresees at the outset the emergence of the conflict, he need refer only one client. If he waits until the conflict is upon him, he may have the pain of referring both. The reason is confidentiality, as we shall see in the next chapter. It goes against the grain for a solicitor to refer a client to another lawyer for at least three reasons. One is purely commercial, the loss of a fee. The second, the risk of loss of the client, is part commercial, part professional. It is professional in part because to most lawyers the size of the client-base is a more important index of achievement than the size of the fee-income. The third reason is wholly professional, the rupture of the lawyer-client bond.

FIFI, LIFO or something else

The acronyms for 'first in first out' and 'last in first out', used for certain tax purposes, are there in the heading to point up the fact that the judgment of which client to refer is not a mechanical one, based on some such formula. Just as confidentiality may impose the obligation to refer both clients, so it may preempt the decision on which one to refer. Once information is taken from one client he is the one who has to be retained. It can well happen that the lawyer is consulted by both clients on the same day on opposite sides of the same matter. The cautious lawyer will not want to operate on the basis of anonymity. Early on, before the client's interest, the pursuit of which will tie him to the client has taken shape, the lawyer should identify that person or those persons who may have a conflicting interest. He then has a choice between clients. This writer was once consulted by client A on a dispute which was about to break out between him and a neighbouring proprietor. The other proprietor was quickly identified at the consultation and turned out to be client B. The decision was to retain client A as the client who had first consulted. In the afternoon of the same day, client B telephoned directly to client A, claiming (falsely) that he had been legally advised that his case was sound and identifying (again falsely, of course), this writer as the source of the advice. Fortunately, client A accepted this writer's denial of client B's assertion. Client B was duly referred to another solicitor. Because of client A's success in the ensuing litigation, client B was encouraged to return.

Loyalty

If not dictated by considerations of confidentiality, how does the lawyer make the invidious choice between clients? Does he always choose the established client in preference to the newly introduced one? Does he select the one with the better, or more intellectually exciting, case? Is he influenced by the extent of the client's dependence, emotionally or otherwise, on his suppport? Does he place greater weight on the probable extent of future work or on the importance of the instant matter? Some of these considerations are obviously commercial and some have ethical resonance. The ethical factor is loyalty. In a contest between commercialism and loyalty, the direction in which the lawyer makes his choice provides a mark for his ethical performance.

Like confidentiality, although not with such imperative force, loyalty may dictate that the lawyer should not act for either of the clients whose interests conflict. The lawyer can recoil, for example, from the prospect of raising an action on behalf of one client against the other. Loyalty in this immediate context is not a matter of professional ethics, as long as confidentiality is not prejudiced. It is hoped that readers will appreciate the distinction between allowing commercial considerations to outweigh loyalty in the choice of the client to be retained (a choice with ethical implications), on the one hand, and allowing dual loyalties to preclude the choice altogether (a decision without ethical implications). Save for the obligation of confidentiality, loyalty in the narrower sense of the loyal pursuit of the client's interest ends with the settlement or completion of the matter. Does loyalty in the broader meaning of a continuing sense of professional responsibility attach to the 'established client' as defined in the Rules on conflict of interest? That definition is mechanical (as it has to be for the purposes of codification). The essential point, we think, is that the client has to earn the lawyer's loyalty. For the first time, we are talking of an obligation of the *client* within the lawyer-client relationship, other than his obligation to pay fees. The reciprocal of continuing loyalty on the lawyer's side is the anticipation of loyalty on the client's side. In relation to the concept of the ethical client, what matters is the loyal client, not the established client. In the previous paragraph, we picked out dependence as one of the factors which may influence choice. His feeling of dependence may or may not underpin a client's loyalty.

Refer to whom

In deciding to whom a client should be referred in order to resolve a conflict of interest problem, the solicitor should look for that practitioner who will *best* pursue the client's interest in that particular matter. Mistrust the lawyer who claims such a degree of saintliness! A formula with a fair mix of pragmatism and ethics is to refer to a lawyer who will do an adequate job for the client, but who lacks the professional charisma to retain him afterwards.

Competence

It takes a conceptual leap to pass from the broad topic of conflict of interest, which has previously occupied us, to a subject like competence. Certainly, it fits legitimately into the purview of a chapter on client's interest and is involved in the last of the questions inherent in the core principle: 'Does "pursue" imply "pursue with competence"?' (cf. p 15). The sense of discordance reflects the difficulty of finding a place for competence within a scheme of professional ethics. On the one hand, the automatic response to our question would almost certainly be a resounding affirmative: the client's interest must be pursued competently by the lawyer. That is his professional responsibility. If his actual performance falls 'deplorably' or 'inexcusably' (for the significance of these criteria, refer back to p 23) below that standard, it would amount to professional misconduct. But on reflection, are such attitudes not reminiscent of the 'punishment' for incompetence in the repetition of the 9 times table, which characterised the 'dark ages' of primary school education? Is a lawyer's incompetence his fault or does it show up imperfections in the system which controls entry into the profession? It is one of the distinguishing marks of a profession that it surrounds itself with a ringfence. This takes the form of a minimum educational qualification as a condition of entry. The incompetent solicitor is one who has been allowed to crawl under, instead of passing through, the ringfence.

Definitions

Incompetence is one thing, professional negligence is something else. The former describes the failure to reach a set standard of performance. The latter is the occasional failure to maintain such a standard. Incompetence is a steady state, negligence a lapse. It is a lapse both from the normal standards of the competent lawyer and the usual standards of that particular, negligent practitioner. It is conceivable that an incompetent lawyer is always negligent (he cannot help but lapse in terms of the normal standards of competent lawyers) or – although less plausibly – never negligent. The Law Society *via* a Competence Committee have produced what they describe as a 'working definition of the competent solicitor' (Appendix 3). We said before (p 13) that competence was a 'dimension'. This is confirmed with blinding clarity by the definition, which would be meaningless without its relativist terms, such as 'appropriate', 'reasonable', 'effective'. The Committee, itself, makes explicit its realisation that its definition would fit the *excellent* solicitor just as well as the *competent* solicitor.

Specialism

Theoretically, a lawyer, who is qualified to practice, may be incompetent in all areas, or in most areas in which he is consulted. No harm is done unless the lawyer actually undertakes the work which he is incomptent to perform. Difficulties in the way of such a desirable, self-denying ordinance by a solicitor are competition for growth in the client base, failure to develop whole-firm specialisation as distinct from specialisation within firms, and the intimacy of the lawyer-client relationship. Fundamentally, the individual lawyer sets out to attract, solve problems and do transactions for, and so satisfy, clients, not to become competent or expert in a circumscribed field of practice. The non-specialist solicitor who, acting properly and altruistically in his client's interest, refers his client not to a speciality firm but to a firm with specialised departments, has grounds to fear that this will represent *adieu* not *au revoir* to his client. (A speciality firm should be defined negatively as a firm which *consistently* turns away all categories of work other than that in which it specialises. The author is aware of only one firm in Scotland which claims to do this.) The large firms with specialised departments have now strongly developed presentational features (not, they would claim, at the expense of substance) seductively associated in the minds of modern consumers – that is all of us – with the choice and consumption of goods.

Reference to counsel

If the disadvantage to a lawyer of reference of his client to another firm of solicitors is the risk involved in parting from a client who has consulted *him*, the risk suffered by the solicitor who consults counsel is damage to the solicitor-client relationship. That is because of ambiguities in the solicitor-counsel process of consultation. Theoretically, a solicitor should consult counsel, in company with his client, in anticipation of litigation or to complete the preparations for the presentation of the case in court. The client ought to have a first-hand analysis of the facts and law and an estimation of his chances from the lawyer who will actually present the case. But counsel often seem to bow to the temptation to pontificate in the form of a second opinion (sometimes no more than a gloss on the solicitor's memorial) rather than to provide a first-hand appraisal. Since the preparation of the case is the solicitor's responsibility, any last-minute deficiencies or necessary improvisations, if loftily pointed out by counsel, become the occasion of further embarrassment for the solicitor. Counsel's role in Scotland is properly that of a specialist pleader of cases prepared by a solicitor. Although he seldom has occasion to develop specialism in a particular area of law, he is not infrequently used by solicitors as a consultant for legal problems. (In England, there is the contrasting position that counsel specialise in particular areas and some seldom plead in court.) Traditionally, the Bar stands above the solicitor branch in the legal hierarchy. This whiff of superiority is fortified by the ceremonial of the consultation. It tends to do damage to the solicitor-client relationship.

Reluctance to refer even within the firm

Naturally, the solicitor will tend to prefer the lesser evil of damage to the solicitor-client relationship to the risk of total loss of the client. He will, therefore, be disposed to consult or instruct counsel rather than refer the client to another solicitor firm with specialist departments. But even *within* such a firm, a strong bond of loyalty and confidence between the client and a particular partner may create resistance to referral. In the case of the referring partner, his reluctance may be reinforced by reservations concerning his specialist partner's personality or aptitude. In the client's case, it may be born of sentiments of loyalty on his part. The conclusion is that the intimacy of the solicitor-client relationship may work against competence in the conditions of increasing complexity and speeded-up responses which create the need for specialism in legal practice.

Competence and ethics

These disincentives to the referral of a client by a solicitor to a specialist are nothing more than psychological in nature. If by yielding to them, the solicitor undertakes work for his client in an area where he is incompetent, he contravenes the ethics of his profession. That does not in itself, however, provide us with an unequivocal answer to the question with which we started. It means no more than that if the lawyer *knows* he is incompetent, he behaves unethically if he does not refer the client. As regards the incompetent lawyer with delusions of competence, we do not have an answer.

Chapter 3

Confidentiality

Confidentiality can be defined as the obligation to keep secret another's confidences and 'confidences' as information which is imparted to or obtained by the confidant on the understanding, express or implied, that it will be kept secret. George Bernard Shaw paradoxically replied to a friend who wanted him to reveal a secret that, while he implicitly trusted the friend, he could not be so sure about the people to whom the friend would be talking. The paradox, of course, originates from the fact that the obligation to keep secrets, where it is not expressed, arises from some trusting relationship such as friendship. At the same time the imparting of secrets, even in breach of confidentiality, creates or fortifies a trusting relationship between confider and confidant. So, psychologic-ally, there is a strong impulse to breach of confidentiality despite the betrayal of trust, at first on a one-to-one basis and then by wider dissemination, the obligation weakening the further it gets from the original source.

Strictest confidence

As a legal duty, the range of confidentiality was explored in a recent English decision (*Stephens v Avery* [1989] 2 All ER 477). The background was the murder trial of a husband who had killed his wife. During the trial, information of the wife's lesbian relationship had emerged. One of the newspapers, in which the story was published, revealed the identity of the other woman in the relationship. She had confided her secret in strictest confidence to someone, who passed it on to a journalist, who, in turn, conveyed it to the newspaper. It was argued that, in the absence either of a legally enforceable contract or a pre-existing relationship, it was not possible to impose a legal duty of confidentiality merely by *saying* that information was imparted in confidence. The judge rejected the argument. Where there was an express imposition of a duty of confidence, he said, the confidant's conscience was as much affected as in the case of the same duty implied by a pre-existing relationship. It was unclear how far down the chain of informers and informants the obligation of confidentiality might travel. There was even a hint that some sort of embryonic right of privacy might be constructed out of this sort of obligation.

Lawyer's obligation and confidentiality

Unlike the obligation to keep a secret in the *Stephens* case which arose from the fact that the information was imparted expressly on the basis that it would not be divulged, the lawyer's like obligation is an attribute of his professional relationship with the client. So far in our analysis of professional ethics, we have managed to derive a system purely from exploration of the core principle that the lawyer pursues the client's interest. Confidentiality, one feels, is not *necessarily* related in that way, however, to the core principle. It is possible to conceive of a system where the lawyer's professional responsibility is to pursue the client's interest but he has no, or only a limited, obligation of confidentiality (although the CCBE Code declares confidentiality to be 'a primary and fundamental right and duty of the lawyer'). As with the lawyer's continuing loyalty to the client (cf. p 56), the obligation of confidentiality is based on an assumption of reciprocity. There is an exchange of confidence or confidences between the lawyer and the client. The client will confide in the lawyer if he is confident that the lawyer will maintain confidentiality. The solicitor-client relationship is fiduciary, a relationship of trust, and its fiduciary character is enhanced by the trusting passage of secrets within it from client to lawyer.

Absence of candour

If the client does not reciprocate, does not keep to his side of the bargain through absence of candour, the lawyer is not, of course, entitled to breach his duty of confidentiality. An absence of candour may mean that the client has given him misleading information or has withheld important information. It is the client's motivation which matters here. A lawyer should possess the skill required to overcome ordinary reticence and stretch the client's perception of what may be relevant. The lawyer may reasonably conclude from the client's absence of candour that it is due to, or has brought about, a breakdown in the professional relationship, so entitling him to terminate it.

Importance of confidentiality

Confidentiality, as we said, provides the basis for the client to entrust his confidences to the lawyer. These are essential for the determination of the client's interest. Although it is the client's perception of his interest which counts, the lawyer should not rely on the client's perception of what disclosures are, or are not, in his interest. The lawyer is better able to differentiate the relevant from the irrelevant, the material from the trivial, the incriminatory from the exculpatory. The potentiality for ethical conflict, for a *crise de conscience*, for the solicitor between confidentiality and the aim of encouraging full disclosure on the one hand and the public interest in a truth-seeking system of justice is evident.

Scope of confidentiality

The obligation extends not just to information emanating from the client but also to all information acquired by the lawyer in the pursuit of the client's interest. Even though information in the latter category is discovered through the lawyer's efforts, owing nothing to the client's confidences to the lawyer, it nevertheless falls within the obligation. It is sometimes thought that matters observed, in contrast to information obtained, by the lawyer (a common example is that the client wore bloodstained clothing when the lawyer saw him) are excepted from the duty of confidentiality (cf. Wilkinson *The Scottish Law of Evidence* (Butterworths, 1986), p 94, where the point is discussed in the context of privilege). This is not the case. Confidentiality would apply to such an observation, although it would not be protected by privilege, the scope of which is narrower.

Duration of confidentiality

The lawyer's problem at the point when conflict of interest arises becomes more awkward, as we said above (cf. p 55), the further the matter has gone with the two clients. That is because the lawyer is precluded from using information confidential to one in the pursuit of the other's interest. Although the solicitor-client relationship may not yet have been established with one of the clients so as to create a conflict of interest problem for the lawyer, any information which he obtains from that client may nonetheless fall within the obligation of confidentiality. Perhaps the best definition of the point in the relationship when the confidentiality first attaches is when the lawyer allows a person to provide him with information in his actual or prospective capacity as lawyer for that person. Even if the lawyer then promptly refuses to act, the information gained up to that point is confidential. Analogously with the *Stephens* case, where the seal of confidentiality was expressly imposed, it attaches in the lawyer-client relationship by implication on the inception of that relationship, as we have defined it.

In the context of conflict of interest, we made the point that a client ceased to be a client, except to the extent that the lawyer retained a sense of continuing loyalty, once the matter was completed. That is not the case with confidentiality. The obligation enures as far as and (subject to the qualifications noted below) beyond the client's death.

Confidentiality and the company lawyer

The dilemma of the company lawyer who hears from an official of his client company that he has engaged in illegal conduct against or on behalf of the company (problem posed on p 47) is puzzling when looked at in relation to confidentiality. One argument would be that the solicitor had allowed him to make the disclosure in his capacity as the company lawyer, not lawyer for the official. As such, the information would be confidential to the company not the official as an individual. As we have conceived it, this looks at the situation from the wrong side, neglecting the official's state of mind and motivation when he made the disclosure. If he did so in good faith and in the reasonable belief that the company lawyer would pursue *his* interest, it could be argued that the confidentiality belonged to the official. In terms of our theory, this is a conflict which can be resolved only in the light of the particular facts and circumstances. One pertinent question, of course, is, in what sense is the lawyer 'the company lawyer'.

Client's consent for disclosure

As we have described it, the obligation of confidentiality has the appearance of a duty owed to, and enforceable by, the client. Such a view is reinforced by our reference in an earlier paragraph to reciprocity by the client. It would seem to follow that, in the event of a breach, a client could, on the model of *Stephens*, ask the court for damages from the lawyer on the ground of his default in an obligation arising from the fiduciary character of the relationship. And so he probably could. Does it follow that the lawyer is free to divulge the information with the client's consent? Some information, indeed, is imparted to the lawyer for the express purpose of its revelation. An accused who confesses to a crime with an instruction to his lawyer to plead guilty provides an example. So does the client who instructs his lawyer to plead poverty on his behalf to defer payment of a debt. At the other end of the range, however, we would consider that a lawyer who released scandalous information concerning his client, even with that client's consent, might have behaved unethically, although the client could not sue him. As an ethical attribute of the relationship, the lawyer undertakes an obligation of confidentiality. It is a condition of his release from that obligation that divulgence should not be detrimental to his client's interest. This is, in our view, another exceptional case where it is the lawyer who is the judge of whether detriment will be caused or not. Both conditions must be met, a judgment of no detriment by the lawyer *and* consent by his client. If the client has since died, the second of the conditions cannot be met. In that event, it would seem that the lawyer would be obliged to keep the client's secret unless he judged that disclosure would be in the client's interest. This amounts to a positive criterion, not mere absence of detriment, a negative one.

Obligations of disclosure

To understand at a deep level the lawyer's ethical duty of confidentiality, one has to see that it forms not just a crossroads, but a veritable spaghetti junction, with three other principles or doctrines. These are: obligations of disclosure, the doctrine of privilege and the legal obligation to the client stemming from the fiduciary character of the relationship. We have already touched on the last of these, when we concluded that it was not coextensive with the lawyer's ethical obliga-tion. When we turn to the relationship between the obligation of confidentiality and obligations of disclosure, there are two ways of regarding it. (In most of this discussion, the distinc-tion between the ethical and the legal obligation of confiden-tiality is immaterial. References to confidentiality can be taken to cover both, except in the case of any reference which is stated to be specific to one.) One can consider the scope of confidentiality to be restricted by the obligation of disclosure so that confidentiality is thought of as attaching to such matters as the lawyer has no obligation to disclose. The alternative view is that confidentiality embraces *all* informa-tion obtained by the lawyer within the lawyer-client relation-ship (this is a shorthand version for present purposes of the more exact definition of its scope in the preceding paragraph) but it is overriden in the case of certain information in certain circumstances by an obligation of disclosure (cf. interchange between Professor Robert Black and P W Ferguson p 71 *post*). (As we shall see, an obligation of disclosure may be legal or ethical in nature.) In this writer's scheme of professional ethics, the latter is the standpoint which has been adopted (cf. p 4 where conflict is taken as the dynamic principle and moral cost as the measure of the loss sustained when one valued duty or objective is overridden by another. Thus, there is an 'ethical cost' when confidentiality is overridden by an obligation of disclosure. This will be evident in the light of the examples given *post*. The problem with the former interpretation is that it becomes impossible to delimit the restricted scope of confidentiality, which results, in any way which is not dogmatic (see the strictures on the American Lawyer's Code relating to this very point at p 8). One might hazard the speculation that the more an exposition of professional ethics aspires to be law-like, the more prone it will be to make a vain attempt at such definition.

Privilege

The doctrine of privilege is part of the law of evidence. It operates as a restriction on the legal obligation of disclosure. Privilege is ubiquitous but its scope varies from jurisdiction to jurisdiction. At one end it is tied in closely to information obtained for the purpose of pending litigation. At the other end it stretches to cover 'all communications properly falling within the scope of the [solicitor-client] relationship' (Wilkinson *The Scottish Law of Evidence* p 94). It would be wrong to conclude from this that privilege is co-extensive with confidentiality. To put the distinction succinctly: privilege protects the lawyer as holder of information from the obligation to disclose it; confidentiality prohibits the lawyer as holder of information from disclosing it. Theoretically, therefore, there may be information which the lawyer is legally obliged to disclose, because it is not protected by privilege, but which he is under an obligation to keep confidential. His observation of his client's bloodstained clothing, which was instanced above (p 64), is a case in point. Given the right circumstances, the lawyer may have come under an obligation of confidentiality with regard to that observed fact. If he is called on to testify to the fact in court, it will not be protected by privilege. Confidentiality will be overriden by the operation of law.

An examination in bankruptcy is a context in which the protection of privilege would be overriden. The Keith Committee, appointed in 1980 to consider changes to statutory

powers backing tax assessment and collection, had recommended that the courts should have power to order disclosure,
in cases involving alleged tax evasion, of information in the
possession of lawyers which would otherwise have been
privileged. The Inland Revenue were reported recently to
have given up their eight-years' campaign to have the recommendation implemented. Had they succeeded, this would
have represented another special case where information
imparted for the purpose of obtaining legal advice was not
privileged. It would, of course, have remained protected by an
enforceable obligation of confidentiality, subject to the
statutory obligation of disclosure.

Interplay

In the sphere of professional ethics, we have to recognise the
entrance of an additional factor. Just as the ethical obligation of
confidentiality goes further than the corresponding legal
obligation, so there may be an ethical obligation of disclosure
as well as a legal one. The interplay among all of these factors
can best be explored by looking at some problem situations.

A question of confidence

In an article under the title 'A Question of Confidence' ((1982)
27 JLSS 299), which is a model of clear and cogent reasoning,
Professor Robert Black examines the predicament of a lawyer
S, to whom X, in the course of a journey 'suddenly and
unexpectedly blurts out' that he, X, committed a particular
robbery about which there had been publicity in the press.
Professor Black's initial conclusion is that the information is
not privileged, not having been obtained by S in pursuit of X's
interest. His test is the same as the one adopted by us above,
having its basis in the informer's motivation or purpose. In the
light of the difference in scope between confidentiality and
privilege, also noted above, Professor Black goes on to consider whether the information might be subject to confidentiality, although not privileged. His criterion here is
whether the information was imparted within the lawyer-

client relationship although not for the purpose of pursuit of the client' interest. He supposes an interesting range of disclosures by a hypothetical client, for example that he had committed adultery or perpetrated a tax fraud and so on. With one exception, the lawyer is being placed by the client in a confessional role. We might have added to the list a hypothetical confession of a lesbian relationship, since Black's analysis of the position of the lawyer as recipient of such information equates it to that of the informant in *Stephens*. (It should perhaps be mentioned here that there is an indication in the article that a Scottish court might not have reached the same conclusion as the English judge in the circumstances of *Stephens*. The article, of course, antedated *Stephens*, but Black doubts whether in Scotland an enforceable obligation of confidentiality can be unilaterally *imposed* on the recipient of information.) What emerges clearly is that the lawyer's confidentiality is no different from that of a priest-confessor, medical practitioner, journalist as regards his sources, or member of MI5 save that, uniquely, the lawyer's information (provided it has been obtained for the purpose of pursuit of the client's interest) has the protection of privilege (a journalist is protected against disclosure of his sources of information under s 10 of the Contempt of Court Act 1981 unless the court is satisfied that disclosure is 'necessary in the interests of justice or national security or for the prevention of disorder or crime').

Public interest

Professor Black then proceeds to make the assumption, unjustified by the facts but purely for the purpose of the ensuing exercise, that S had become subject to an obligation of confidentiality of the *Stephens* type. If he then breached the confidence by reporting X as the perpetrator of a serious crime to the authorities, would he be vulnerable to court action by X in the same way as the informant was in *Stephens*? Professor Black shows that S – in contrast to the *Stephens* informant – would be entitled to 'the public policy defence'. The public interest in knowing of the commission of a serious crime and the identity of the person who had committed it justifies the disclosure in breach of confidentiality. As we indicated above, the term 'justification' is apt, as Professor Black says, to cover, two possible meanings: either the public interest constitutes a defence to the breach of an obligation; or no obligation existed at all since there cannot be a lawful obligation to keep such information confidential. The latter is Professor Black's preferred view. (The question of whether privilege dies with the client is also raised. That is not automatic. But Black considers that the balance of authority indicates that the court would order disclosure of this sort of information after X's death even though it had been privileged before).

Public interest v confidentiality

A slippery distinction lies between what we will now call professional confidentiality, that is the obligation arising in relation to information received by the lawyer for the purpose of his giving legal advice or, as we put it, for the purposes of pursuit of the client's interest, on the one hand, and *Stephens*-type confidentiality on the other. *Stephens*-type confidentiality, as we saw, can also arise as a result of the lawyer-client relationship, which takes the place of the express imposition or acceptance of an obligation to keep a secret in the layman's case. Without doubt, professional confidentiality would oblige S not to reveal X's confession. *Stephens*-style confidentiality would not prevent S from making such disclosure. In an interchange of comment and reply between Ferguson and Black (this appeared under the same heading 'A Question of Confidence' in (1982) 27 JLSS 390), the further issue was raised, whether S, in a *Stephens*-style situation, had a positive obligation of disclosure. Apart from special statutory provisions, there is no legal obligation on any citizen 'to volunteer information regarding past criminal conduct to the police or to the prosecuting authorities'. Sheriff Gordon (*Criminal Law*, W Green & Son, 2nd edn, 1978, para 48.40) was quoted:

'There is no authority for saying that Scotland is a police state in which every man is bound to inform on his neighbour.'

The discussion then inevitably went on to consider whether there was an ethical obligation of disclosure. Now we come into the realm of moral conflict. The duty to divulge the information might override the obligation to keep it secret. It might amount to a breach of professional ethics not to reveal the information. It might go against professional ethics, on the other hand, not to maintain its confidential nature. As Black says, it depends on circumstances such as the gravity of the crime, how far in the past it was committed, the circumstantial pressure on the lawyer to tell the truth and so on.

Public interest v professional confidentiality

It is difficult, if not impossible, to conceive of circumstances in which public interest can justifiably override professional confidentiality (in making this assertion, we must strictly distinguish public interest considerations from universal values: see p 4 and *post*). One way of rationalising such a statement is to say that there is such a strong public interest in the system of justice and professional confidentiality is of such crucial importance for that system that it outweighs all other public policy considerations. The marginal case is the prevention of future or continuing crimes, a problem area which has worried the framers of the American codes.

Future and continuing crimes

It is obvious that a lawyer cannot advise with regard to a crime about to be perpetrated. If he is consulted in such circumstances no obligation of confidentiality will arise. A lawyer acting in the capacity of a tax planning adviser must be vigilant not to recommend or participate in a scheme which oversteps the boundary between avoidance (lawful) and evasion (criminal). But if the lawyer is not consulted with regard to the future crime, the circumstances are likely to be such that he will be placed under nothing more than a *Stephens*-style confidentiality obligation, over which the public interest considerations discussed in the preceding paragraph may justifiably prevail. It is appropriate now to complete Dershowitz's battle cry (see p 10) in which he asserts his single-minded aim 'to get [his] client off'. He adds:

'I do not apologise for (or feel guilty about) helping to let a murderer go free – even though I realise that some day one of my clients may go out and kill again.'[1]

It is perhaps too easy to wave aside the defence lawyer's dilemma with the argument that anxiety about the potentiality of a future murder by his client is purely speculative. If we suppose, though, that the client is a known member of the IRA, the ethical conflict acquires more substance. The comment by one of the government's junior ministers recently reported in the press to the effect that lawyers for the IRA were 'unduly sympathetic' to their clients is discussed in Chapter 6. Nevertheless, in relation to professional confidentiality, it cannot be said that even strong qualms of conscience stemming from a public duty to prevent crimes will permit the lawyer to break his obligation of confidentiality.

Universal values v professional confidentiality

It hardly needed to be said that professional confidentiality must be dominant over the public interest in a truth-seeking system of justice. Nor can the high value accorded to truth-telling be allowed to make incursions into that obligation of the lawyer, even if the consequence is personal embarrassment or the appearance of dishonesty (it is appreciated that the need to subordinate truth-telling or even candour may reflect adversely on the image of the profession. Breach of professional confidentiality would, however, be worse in that respect). The caring attitude towards human life, though, which is perhaps the hallmark of a civilised society, is another matter. The American Lawyer's Code exempts the lawyer from his obligation of confidentiality where divulgence is 'necessary to prevent imminent danger to human life'. So formulated, this strikes us as a somewhat smug ignoring of realities in order to produce the appearance of a law out of a

---

1 This is fully analysed along with Dershowitz's analogy of the surgeon who saves the life of a patient who later kills an innocent victim in this author's *The Lawyer and Society* (Ardmoray Publishing 1987) pp 187–9.

whole continuum of ethically worrying situations. There can be occasions when his estimation of how realistic is a threat, how imminent is a danger, how life-threatening is an injury, how deep is a suicidal depression, will push the tender-minded lawyer one way and the tough-minded lawyer the other. Every lawyer must hope to avoid such an incident where the maintenance of profesional confidentiality involves a serious risk of loss of life or extreme suffering. If it occurs, the American Lawyer's Code formula will not help him.

Obligation of disclosure to retained clients

In a conflict of interest situation which has to be resolved by reference to another solicitor of one of the clients whose interests conflict, we have noted previously that a problem of confidentiality remains (p 55). This supposes a clash between the duty of confidentiality owed to the departing client and the lawyer's professional obligation to the retained client. Is there necessarily then an obligation of disclosure to the remaining client? An affirmative answer would lead to an impasse. There is no way in which one obligation can be satisfied without the other's breach. Nor does there seem to be any ethical basis on which the lawyer can discriminate between his two mutually exclusive duties. One satisfactory way out of the lawyer's predicament would seem to be for him to obtain the ex-client's consent to divulgence, provided that the other condition already noted can also be fulfilled, namely that the lawyer conscientiously considers that disclosure of the information would not be detrimental to the ex-client's interest. Once a situation has arisen, however, which makes it necessary or even desirable for the client to have separate legal representation, that route is blocked. If then access to information pertinent to the pursuit of the remaining client's interest is obstructed by the obligation of confidentiality to the other, the lawyer must refer both clients.

Husband and wife

In the breakdown of a marriage, the irony that the spouses' solicitor may know more about the financial (not to mention extra-marital) affairs of each than either does of the other's puts the lawyer on the spot. This may be complicated by the fact that one spouse knows more about the other's affairs than the other knows that he or she knows. In certain circumstances, too, knowledge of a solicitor may be imputed to the client (the most recent authority known to the writer is the English case *Strover v Harrington* [1988] 1 All ER 769). Add in these ingredients: that warring spouses are often on the lookout for a scapegoat; that the 'family solicitor' is well fitted for that part; and that the spouse referred elsewhere may well feel doubly rejected. Strain off the moral argument that each spouse's financial doings should have been open to the other. You then have a witches' brew, which the lawyer, in making the decision whether to act for one of the spouses, should be wary of imbibing.

Self-interest and confidentiality

One piece of apparently nondescript information which is definitely covered by the cloak of confidentiality is the client's whereabouts. Sometimes the client, for one reason or another, lays an express obligation of non-disclosure on the lawyer. Whether this has happened or not, the obligation of confidentiality applies just the same. (To show that his reticence is for good professional reasons and not mere truculence, the lawyer should offer to forward any communication.) What should the lawyer do if the client owes him a fee which the client persistently refuses to pay? If he takes proceedings to enforce payment of the fee, he runs the risk of revealing his client's address. The lawyer can fairly argue that, in defaulting in this way, the client has forfeited his right to withhold consent to the revelation. The lawyer can proceed then without compunction against the client, provided that he is reasonably sure that the disclosure of the client's whereabouts will not have adverse consequences for the client. What if he is sure of the opposite? The framers of the American Lawyer's Code reject what they state to be a previously recognised exception permitting lawyers to violate confidentiality to collect an unpaid fee. They justify the new position by the argument that the lawyer's financial interest is not suffiently weighty to override the impairment of confidentiality. In principle, one would be inclined to support that view. In making a judgment, though, in a particular case one would want to consider several possible factors: the importance of the fee to the lawyer's finances; the reason that the fee is unpaid, opportunism on the client's part, lack of funds, unfounded criticism of the lawyer's performance; the nature of the harm which may ensue for the client in consequence of the disclosure; the extent of the risk of such harm. Again, the crux is the extent of mutuality in the solicitor-client relationship. Is there an exchange of confidence? If the client betrays the lawyer's confidence in him, is the lawyer not then justified in opening up a small breach in the confidentiality owed to the client?

A final problem

A lawyer has acted regularly for a client, A, in the purchase and leasing out of parts of an investment property. He is consulted by client B, for whom he has also acted regularly, who tells him that he has arranged to take a let of some office space in client A's building. The last matter handled by the lawyer for client B was his defence on a charge of arson. In the course of the defence, the lawyer found reason to believe that the client had acquired some unsavoury connections. The defence was unsuccessful, client B was convicted and now, after a spell in prison, requires the office to give him a fresh start in business. Will the lawyer act for him in the lease transaction? The lawyer takes the easy way out of telling him that he is professionally precluded from acting for both parties in a commercial lease (see p 43) and refrains from referring him to another solicitor.

He is exercised, though, by the problem of whether he has a duty of disclosure concerning client B's fire-raising episode to client A, the prospective landlord. He postpones this unpleasant decision on the safe assumption that he will be given instructions to conclude missives *before* the landlord has otherwise committed himself to the lease. If he does receive such instructions, what should he do? There are reasonable grounds for believing that his ex-client (ex-client, but he still owes him a duty of confidentiality) is an unsuitable tenant. He has to take into account that the building insurance, which he has arranged, is a contract *uberrimae fidei*. His knowledge concerning the new tenant's past record may constitute a ground for invalidation of the policy, either because he is in bad faith by failing to disclose it to the insurance company or because it is imputed to his client, the landlord, with the same effect.

The question which he turns over in his mind is whether, since the criminal conviction is deemed to be public knowledge, that absolves him from any revelatory duty. What stops him from drawing complete reassurance from this, though, is an argument of Lord Keith in the Spycatcher case[2] where he draws an analogy from an action brought by the Duchess of Argyll against the Duke[3] to show that a duty of confidentiality can still be breached even where the information is public. What he said (at p 640) was: 'For example if in the *Argyll* case the Duke had secured the revelation of the marital secrets in an American newspaper, the Duchess could reasonably claim that publication of the same material in England would bring it to the attention of people who would otherwise be unlikely to learn of it and who were more closely interested in her activities than American readers. The publication in England would be more harmful to her than publication in America'.

2 *Attorney General v Guardian Newspapers Ltd (No 2)* [1989] 3 All ER 638, HL.
3 *Margaret, Duchess of Argyll v Duke of Argyll* [1965] 1 All ER 611, [1967] Ch 302.

Chapter 4

The adversarial system

In this chapter we bring into focus the impact of the adversarial system on professional ethics. How is the practice of law viewed from an ethical standpoint affected by the fact that the lawyer has to pursue the client's interest within the framework of an adversarial system (for an analysis of adversarialism in transactions and cases see p 34 *ante*)?

Soviet procuracy

For empirical confirmation that professional ethics are affected by the nature of the system, we can look at an area of the Soviet legal system, as lawyers there struggle to reform the legal process within the great movement towards *glasnost* – the opening-up of procedures hitherto shrouded in secrecy – and *perestroika* – the restructuring of organisations and redistribution of power within them[1]. The decision of the procuracy (the organisation of prosecutors) to bring the case to trial verged, Professor Fletcher observed, on an official finding that the defendant was guilty. The prestige of the procuracy exceeded that of the court itself. The Soviet defence lawyer is permitted to see his client for the first time only at the end of the preliminary investigation and after the client has been held in preventive detention, subject to regular interrogation, for a period which may exceed one year. As a result, the most effective intervention by the defence lawyer is likely to be immediately pre-trial when, after reading the investigator's

---

1 This summary is based on an article 'In Gorbachev's Court' by Professor Fletcher, an American professor of law, in the New York Review of Books on 18 May 1989. He had made a close-up study of an ordinary criminal trial on a visit to the Soviet Union as a member of a Helsinki Watch mission.

dossier, he can try to persuade the investigator to reduce the charges or dismiss the case for want of proof. Soviet lawyers do not interview witnesses in preparation for the trial. To do that would be a breach of professional ethics. The procuracy's function is to investigate 'objectively' both sides of the case. If the defence lawyer were to conduct a private interview of a witness, he would be likely to distort that witness's testimony. (It is a recognised principle in our jurisdiction that those who plead in the higher courts should not also have been involved in the investigating of the evidence. But investigation, of course, is in such cases the task of the defence solicitors or, in civil cases, the party's solicitor). This was the present picture, but Soviet lawyers were now actively pushing for the introduction of adversarialism into the system.

Lawyer's roles

Professor Fletcher perceives the Soviet criminal defence lawyer as acting 'as the loyal opposition to an official investigation dominated by the prosecutor'. On the face of it, this bears quite a strong similarity to the view of lawyers as 'ombudsmen, who serve the system as much as they serve clients' (cf. p 10; see relationship of this view to independence of the legal profession, Chapter 6). Both could qualify as a 'collectivist, bureaucratic concept' (the American Lawyer's Code's words for the Kutak Commission's view). Each encapsulation of the lawyer's 'true' role in society, as 'loyal opposition', 'ombudsman', 'citizens' champion against official tyranny' (the last being the American Lawyer's Code's chosen role-ideal), both generates and reflects different ethical approaches or emphases. The adversarial system can accommodate, as we shall see, both the ombudsman and the citizens' champion functions.

Partisanship

In an adversarial system, each interest which presents itself to be pursued by the lawyer is defined in terms of an actually or potentially conflicting interest. The lawyers who represent the interests in issue are pitted against each other in an adversarial relationship. They conduct their dealings in a partisan way.

Rules of the contest

Even conflictive relationships are 'law-making' in the sense that they generate rules, the main purpose of which is to separate the permissible means of conducting the relationship from the impermissible. In *The Lawyer and Society* pp 200 *et seq*, this process was explored in relation to the rules of a game or contest. Although these were nowhere written down or, even if they were, were hardly ever read, they were so firmly grasped not only by the players or contestants but also by the spectators that the use of impermissible means would bring forth a concerted shout of 'foul'. (Similarly, in the war with Iran, the use of chemical weapons by Iraq was generally regarded by the global spectators as a contravention of a rule appropriate to such conflict. Some of the Arab countries were stung into countering with the argument that if a nuclear weapon had been used instead, even though it would have caused greater loss of life, more distressing long-term injuries and more widespread contamination, it might not have been regarded in the same way.)

Fair means and foul

The recognition that all-out conflict should not be all-in crept, as we saw, into Dershowitz's battle-hymn for the zealous lawyer:

'Once I decide to take a case, I have only one agenda! I want to win. I will try, by every *fair and legal means*, to get my client off – without regard to the consequences' (author's italics). The self-denying renunciation of 'unfair means' seems at first sight to be incongruous in the context of his *ruat caelum* (reckless of the consequences) approach. But it reflects his acknowledgment that lines have to be drawn to mark the boundaries of the permissible. The sense of what is fair or unfair develops into understanding of the special nature of the particular conflict or contest. The limits of fair tackling are different in soccer and rugby and different again in American football. If we use that as a metaphor, just what constitutes fair tackling in a contest between lawyers is a highly complex matter. The lawyers who play have a keen sense of what it is because they are immersed day-in day-out in the same patterns of moves. Clients are not like spectators or fans. They have a closer involvement in the outcome, but little appreciation of the finer points of the moves which determine it. They are like people who have placed such heavy bets on a result that the need or desire to win chokes off interest in anything other than the *effectiveness* of the moves.

Professional etiquette and other appearances

Foul or unfair means or impermissible moves are different in character from meaningless actions. To kill prisoners-of-war, to smash the opponent's chess pieces when they have been removed from the board, to kick the ball into the crowd, are obviously meaningless. They are pointless so far as the achievement of the objective is concerned. But just because they are pointless, and especially because they represent pointless expressions of aggression, they are disturbing in a particular way. They are a threat. Although slight in themselves in practical importance, they seem to symbolise outright rejection of the spirit of the game. They are not breaches of the rules in the sense of fouls or unfair means. They break with the ceremonial of the contest, disrupt the solemnity of the occasion. (See *The Lawyer and Society* pp 108 *et seq* for an analysis of the three functions of solemnity in the legal process; cf. the Victorian judge's outburst in face of such a breach of ceremonial 'I cannot abide arguments addressed to me by counsel whose legs are encased in tight, grey-check trousers,' taken from *The Websters.*) If we set these observations in the context of legal process, we find ourselves at a fair distance from the core of the lawyer-client relationship, the pursuit of the client's interest. We have been talking about the outward trappings, what is or used to be called professional etiquette (fully discussed in Chapter 5).

Fair outcomes

Fair comment on the Victorian judge's behaviour would have been that he should have concentrated more on the arguments and less on the trousers. The same point, in terms of our generic contest, would be brought out by the proposition that no game can be understood without an appreciation of what the players are struggling to achieve. What is the goal – or the equivalent of a goal – which determines who has won or who has played well? That is not to be judged by appearances or by the fairness of moves. (In *The Glass Bead Game*, a novel by Hesse, the whole culture of an isolated society was occupied with the playing of the glass bead game. The game was never described – such a game would have been indescribable – but it represented the ultimate in intellectual refinement with strong suggestions of spiritual overtones. The atmosphere of the society absorbed in the game was hushed, saintly, bloodlessly unemotional. Ultimately, one came to see it as over-refined, a society whose resources of intellectual skill were devoted to a game, whose aesthetic and ethical values related to the beauty and rightness of the moves of the game – a game without an end or conclusion, without a winner or a loser, without spectators who could appreciate its finer points.) Due process and, corresponding to that, fair means are necessarily a strong concern of those who play a part in the legal system. But do those players have any responsibility to achieve fair outcomes? For Dershowitz, it will be remembered, there was an easy answer. He would strive to get his client off. The American Lawyer's Code, as we saw, depicts the (trial) lawyer's goal as the defence of the citizen 'against official tyranny'. There is no indication in either of those declarations of objectives of any concern with fair outcomes. But when lawyers are portrayed as 'ombudsmen of the system' (see p 10), that suggests a different attitude. In the rest of this chapter, we will try to show in what manner and to what extent the pursuit of the client's interest within the framework of an adversarial system involves the lawyer in a commitment to both fair means and fair outcomes.

Litigation

Uncertainty of outcome

In litigation, the outcome is in a sense imposed. Its relationship to the quality of the performances which have preceded it is certainly complex, even if not obscure. The folklore says that good advocates do not win cases, bad advocates lose them. But it is impossible to know. A judge, as a connoisseur, may see fit to give the advocate on the losing side the consolation prize of an acknowledgment in his judgment of the intellectual quality of his presentation of the argument. The client who has suffered perhaps a just, but not a fair, outcome of his case will find no solace there.

Never stir up litigation

An admonition to that effect is contained in the International Bar Association's International Code of Ethics (adopted in 1956 and from time to time amended). In that negative form, as the Code itself recognises, it is too bland and uncontroversial to be of much help. To what extent should the lawyer try to discourage his client from litigation? On the one hand, there is a public interest in the provision of access to the system of justice for everyone. The grand universality of such a proposition has to be scaled down, though, to fit the limits imposed by the available facilities. Should it be everyone with a *probabilis causa*, then? (This is the criterion on the basis of which legal aid is awarded.) There is at least as strong a countervailing public interest in keeping litigation down to a minimum. Public policy has to reconcile the two conflicting interests as best it can. The lawyer, in pursuit of his client's interests, should not allow himself to be swayed by either.

Contingency fees

Since the advocate knows that he cannot *ensure* that his adversary will not win the case, he has an obligation to attempt to predict the outcome for his client. On the basis of such a prediction, the lawyer should, nearly always (an exception would be where the client was slow to grasp a clear weakness in the adversary's case), urge a low-risk strategy on his client. As a hired gun (cf. p 38) the American attorney is notoriously more trigger-happy than his UK equivalent. Of course, it is impossible to say whether the trigger-happiness is a quality of the lawyer or the client. The contingency fee arrangement, under which the lawyer in the US contracts to receive a substantial percentage of the proceeds in the event of success and no fee on failure, gives him a personal stake in the litigation. This is bound to make him more prone, as something of a joint venturer, to adopt, in conjunction with his client, a higher-risk strategy. The lawyer's direct, personal involvement in the client's interests represents a distortion of the lawyer-client relationship as we see it. There are two facets to the contingency fee arrangement. The lawyer charges no, or a reduced, fee in the event of the failure. In the case of success, the lawyer charges an enhanced fee, sometimes proportionately related to the result (this is the norm in contingency fee arrangements in the US). In Scotland, there is no ban or discouragement in respect of arrangements of the first kind. But an enhanced fee in the event of success is forbidden. In England, champertous arrangements are prohibited[2]. The prohibition certainly extends to enhanced fees in the event of success and the author understands, although it is a matter of interpretation, that, unlike Scotland, reduced fees are also covered by the prohibition. The CCBE Code provides that a lawyer is not entitled to make a 'pactum de quota litis'. This it defines as an agreement 'by virtue of which the client undertakes to pay the lawyer a share of the result'. In the Green Paper (The Scottish Legal Profession: the way forward), the government has put out for consultation a proposal that contingency fee arrangements might be introduced into the UK legal systems in some form. This would clash with the CCBE Code.

---

2 Champerty is the name given to contingency fee deals with clients.

Disclosure of adverse law

The system depends on partisan presentation by each side. But it also requires adherence to the rules which articulate the philosophy underlying the system. Take, for example, the principle that an advocate should draw the court's attention to a materially relevant decision, no matter how hostile it is to his client's case. This can be supported by expediency. If he introduces it, it suggests that his argument can survive it; it gives him the chance to make accommodating distinctions. But the argument from expediency is not totally convincing. Neither his opponent nor the judge may come across the decision independently. Do we express the ethical point by saying that the obligation to the court to reveal the adverse case-decision overrides the duty to the client, which might well be better served by its non-disclosure? Or is it preferable to say, instead, that the former obligation is inherent in the adversarial framework within which the client's interest is to be pursued? The latter seems right. When the client instructs court action he submits, and forces his opponent to concede or, if not, also to submit, to the legal system. The legal system articulates the law in response to the imperative to maintain the integrity of the law. This in turn demands that *all* the relevant law is brought to bear on each particular issue.

The court finds the facts

The system makes no such demand on the lawyer so far as the fact-finding task of the court is concerned. For accuracy of evidence, the court relies on rigorous cross-examination. The lawyer's stand in relation to his client should be that it is in his client's interests to tell him the truth. Underlying that stand are elements of expediency, morality and professional ethics. Most lawyers take it as given that to confide fully in them is in the client's interest. In the face of certain situations, such as a criminal charge or bankruptcy proceedings, where the client's veracity will be in question and his answers to the lawyer's questions are shifty, the lawyer may conduct a mock cross-examination from a hostile standpoint. If information emanating from the client is suspect in a different sort of context, say, in the case of a dispute concerned with the terms actually agreed between the landlord and the tenant for a commercial lease, the testing of the information has to be carried out much more circumspectly.

Passing information

The general principle is that a solicitor is not responsible for information given him by a client and provided to another on the client's behalf. In a recent case Lord Jauncey observed (in *Midland Bank plc v Cameron, Thom, Peterkin & Duncans* 1988 SLT 611) that, in the absence of an express assumption of responsibility by the solicitor, what would count would be (1) if he let it be known that he claimed, by reason of his calling, to have the requisite knowledge to furnish the information; (2) if the recipient of the information had relied upon it as matters for which the solicitor had assumed personal responsibility; and (3) if the solicitor was aware that the recipient was likely so to rely. The case was concerned with whether the solicitor owed a duty of care to a third party (here, a bank) in respect of information passed on, and on which the third party had allegedly relied to its detriment. Apart from the question of legal liability, however, a solicitor would not want, as a matter of ordinary morality, to be used as a channel for misstatements by a client. If freedom from legal responsibility becomes a basis for irresponsibility towards the factual accuracy of statements made on the client's behalf, the lawyer himself will lose credibility. Where anything seems dubious or inconsistent, the client should be quizzed. There should be no fudging or deliberate ambiguity as to the source of the information. Introductory phrases like 'We are satisfied that . . .' or 'The fact is that . . .' put the solicitor's personal integrity on the line. The imprimatur implied by inclusion in a solicitor's letter, however, should not be lost, as it will be if the solicitor expressly dissociates himself from the material or allows any note of scepticism to creep into it. He should write as if he believed what he had been told.

False information

In the last paragraph, we were discussing information, whose source is the client and which is untestable or which the solicitor is not under any obligation to verify. But it is a firm principle that a lawyer should not advance any information which he *knows* to be false, an obligation which can extend to cover the concealment of material in whose absence something would be taken for granted. The extent to which a lawyer can turn a blind eye or a deaf ear depends on how 'knowledge' is defined. The definition in the American Lawyer's Code is as follows:

'A lawyer knows certain facts, or acts knowingly or with knowledge of facts, when a person with that lawyer's professional training and experience would be reasonably certain of those facts in view of all the circumstances of which the lawyer is aware. A duty to investigate or enquire is not implied by the use of the words . . .'

In this area, the lawyer may well encounter difficulty in escaping from the conflict between the client's interest, the truth-seeking goal of the system of justice and the moral commitment to the truth. Dershowitz's stance is characteristically robust: 'at all costs to prevent the truth coming out'. But a lawyer cannot sit by and allow his client to commit perjury. The solution to the problem truly lies in philosophy. Unless the lawyer has been a participant or observer, he is in no position to *know* the facts. After the event, the facts are as the court finds them (see *The Lawyer and Society* pp 85 *et seq* for a fuller discussion). The problem of retracted confessions by clients, which seems theoretically vexing, will normally resolve itself in practice. In the last analysis, the lawyer has no way of *knowing* whether the confession or the retraction corresponds to the facts.

Client's withholding of confidences

As a result of the sheer closeness of the lawyer–client relationship, the system of professional ethics applies to virtually all of the lawyer's communings with and conduct towards the client. That is not reciprocal, the client has no *professional* responsibility. But, whether on grounds of ordinary morality or expediency, the client owes something to the relationship. In the light of the lawyer's obligation of confidentiality, the client should entrust the lawyer with his confidences. Here we meet the counterpart of the psychological problem of counselling. There the lawyer is troubled by a plethora of disclosures, here he may be impeded by the client's reticence, bred from shame, embarrassment or misplaced loyalties. Most importantly, the failure to trust the lawyer may be not for psychological reasons nor due to inability to distinguish the relevant from the irrelevant, but the result of calculation. If the client is aware, or senses and is afraid, of the lawyer's obligation not knowingly to advance false information, he may choose to suppress important facts or to answer questions with evasions and half-truths.

Lawyer's response to false information

How does the lawyer respond to a client's withholding of confidence? In the first place, he has failed, perhaps through no fault of his own, in the creation of the atmosphere of trust essential to enable him to take instructions. The first step in that process is to assemble the facts. Moving on, his advice and the strategy adopted to deal with the client's problem may turn out to be built on sand if the true facts emerge. The case may collapse in court, he may be reduced to speechlessness in negotiations with the opponent's solicitors, he may misguidedly make a damaging admission. Breach by the client of his obligation in this way entitles the lawyer to terminate the agency. He cannot do that, however, if the effect of his withdrawal would be materially damaging to his client's interest. That would be the case, for example, where the lawyer anticipates that he would be forced to explain his withdrawal and as a result would be involved in a breach of his obligation of confidentiality. Paradoxically, the client's failure to place confidence in the lawyer does *not* relieve the latter of his duty of confidentiality to the client.

Undertakings by lawyers

In the preceding sections, we have discussed the lawyer's concern for the integrity of the law which requires him to present his client's case within the framework of the whole body of relevant doctrine, whether favourable or not, and also his more equivocal concern with the facts. In the latter context, Lord Jauncey had laid down the criteria which would determine whether a solicitor would be held responsible under the law of reparation for loss suffered by a third party through misstatements derived from his client and transmitted by him to that third party. The discussion was intended, however, to focus on ethical obligations and commitments, not law. When we pass from law and facts to undertakings by lawyers, the law – this time largely of contract – again comes in but our emphasis must remain on ethics.

It is accepted by solicitors that letters of obligation, which cover the period of risk between the dates to which searches can be brought down and the recording or registration dates of titles to interests in land, represent personal commitments by the solicitors who grant them, unless, that is, they are expressly granted on behalf of clients. Indeed, they meet Lord Jauncey's criteria for determining that responsibility has been personally assumed by the solicitor. The solicitor, though, is under no *legal* obligation to enter into such a commitment. It is understood as a matter of professional ethics, however, that the solicitor should replace the client's contractual obligation with one of his own, in pursuit of his client's interest in having punctual settlement, unless he considers that the risk is too great.

Integrity of the conveyancing system

There are two factors underlying the convention that it is ethically incumbent on the solicitor to give a letter of obligation. One is the profession's collective responsibility for the integrity of the conveyancing system. To particularise, the solicitor who acts for the grantee of an interest in land considers himself bound not to release his client's money to the granter except in exchange for the documentary means whereby his client can safely achieve a secure title to the interest. Included in that documentation, therefore, has to be the letter of obligation by the granter's solicitor. In the old days, 'exchange' meant literally a hand-to-hand interchange of a pile of documents and papers for a sum of money, like the handing of cash over a shop counter in exchange for goods. Just as the solicitor's letter of obligation in replacement of the client's contractual obligation was taken to represent the safe route to a secure title, so the other solicitor's cheque instead of his client's cheque was accepted as the equivalent of cash. Nowadays, there is much less insistence on literal exchange at face-to-face settlement but much greater emphasis on the form of payment. Many settlements are carried out by post, so that reliance is placed on the first recipient solicitor not to take title or cash a cheque until he has fulfilled his side of the exchange. The fiction of constructive non-delivery is adopted. The recipient holds what he has received as agent of the sender. But, at the same time as there is less formality about exchange, there is greater strictness about what constitutes payment. Cleared funds, not solicitor's cheques, are progressively a more frequent requirement, not necessarily or ostensibly because of doubt whether the latter will be met, but because of greater awareness of the value of money in times of high interest rates.

Breaches of ethics

To put a stop on payment of a cheque handed over at settlement or to pass a cheque at settlement without funds in the bank to meet it, even though a back-up cheque expected from the client has not arrived or has failed to clear, is a blatant breach of professional ethics. By the same token, so would be the recording or registration of, or founding on, a deed held as undelivered. More subtle is the case of a refusal to give a letter of obligation for a trustworthy client. There is no legal obligation, nor would it amount to professional misconduct, not to provide a letter of obligation in such circumstances, but it must, according to our conception, be reckoned to be a breach of professional ethics.

Reciprocity of trust

The other reason – other that is than the maintenance of the system's integrity and the smoothing out of its operation – for personal commitments by the solicitor is the reciprocity of trust underlying the lawyer-client relationship. Each assumes that he can safely place confidence in the other. The client understands that the lawyer makes common cause with him in that it is his (the client's) interest which is pursued. The common cause makes it necessary that the lawyer should be able to rely on the client's statements and assurances. The client has to appreciate that the routines of the adversarial system limit, even define, the ways in which his interest is pursued.

Duty to third parties arising from undertakings

A recent English case (*Al-Kandari v J R Brown & Co* [1987] 2 WLR 469) showed that when the solicitor gave an undertaking, although his obligation was personal in the sense that it was his and not his client's, it might stretch to protect anyone who came within the category of 'neighbour' in the *Donoghue v Stevenson* (1932 SLT 317, 1932 SC (HL) 31) sense. The circumstances in which the solicitor's undertaking was provided were that the solicitor's client had consented to an order of the court allowing custody of the children to his plaintiff wife with access to himself, a condition being that he lodged his passport, which included the children, with his solicitor. The solicitor was tricked into letting the passport out of his control, as a result of which the husband obtained possession of it and used it to abduct the children and take them out of the country. The Court of Appeal held that the solicitor had breached a duty owed not to his client but to his client's opponent. The solicitor's liability was founded on tort. What is important from our standpoint is that the law on tort or delict is largely concerned with a circumscribed complex of blameworthy acts and omissions. Ethical obligations occupy the same territory. The solicitor in the *Al-Kandari* case, we would say, was, therefore, blameworthy also from the point of view of professional ethics (although, as Lord Donaldson MR said in his judgment, there was no suspicion of any misconduct on the solicitor's part). From that viewpoint, the proximity of the opponent to the solicitor on the other side arises from the network of interaction within the adversarial system.

Solicitor's word should be his bond

So far we have been dealing with formal undertakings given in a context where responsibility is assumed by the granters and other persons are justified in their reliance on them. It is trite law, however, that not every undertaking or promise is binding even where there is acceptance by the other party. My word is not necessarily my bond. As the law at present stands, this is not just a matter of evidence, arising from the difficulty of proof that someone has given his word and meant it. Some obligations require formality for their very constitution – notoriously those relating to heritable property. For the ethical solicitor, his word, if given without equivocation or qualification, even in the absence of formality, is his bond. That is so, even in a situation where the word is being given clearly on behalf of his client. It follows that a situation can arise where the solicitor has committed the client informally to a contract to which the client need not legally adhere due to the lack of the necessary formality. Typically, what is the position of the solicitor acting for the seller of a house who seeks to gazump the purchaser after the solicitor has, with his authority, 'committed' him informally to the sale, but before the missives have been concluded? The seller is, of course, free in law to take the higher offer and the solicitor is bound so to advise him. In our sketch, however, the client, by dint of his authorisation of the solicitor to enter into the commitment to the purchaser, is *morally* bound to keep his word. It is part of the solicitor's professional duty, we conceive it, while advising him of his legal entitlement to withdraw, to attempt to persuade him not to exercise that right. If the solicitor fails in that endeavour, the argument from the side of professional ethics must be that the solicitor's position is untenable if he has truly 'committed' the client. What, while falling short of a contractual obligation, would constitute such a 'commitment'? It is arguable that there can *ex hypothesi* be no such 'commitment', since the purchaser's solicitor to whom the informal communication is made knows very well that without formality there is no legal commitment. The correct view is suggested to be that, if there is a mutual understanding between both solicitors that agreement *has* been reached on all points and its reduction to writing is a *mere* formality, the seller's solicitor, or indeed the purchaser's solicitor if *his* client sought not to proceed, is *professionally* compromised. He should terminate the professional relationship provided that his client's interest does not suffer through the termination. (This, it has to be said, may be a minority view. There is the point that the solicitor has manufactured his own problem through his own incaution. The most cogent argument on the other side is that the client should recognise and respond appropriately to his lawyer's predicament, once the lawyer explains that the client's repudiation of his instructions will cause the lawyer to lose professional credibility.)

Negotiation

All but what must be only a tiny percentage of problems and disputes are resolved by negotiation not litigation. Litigation is dramatic and so is war a dramatic form of struggle. Clausewitz (On War) said that war was just diplomacy carried on by other means. Analogously, a valid perspective on litigation is that it is continuance of negotiation in another form. Until the judge gives his decision, and even after that until the outcome of the final appeal, the parties or their lawyers may negotiate a settlement of their dispute. The lawyer's role in negotiation is perhaps even more crucial than in litigation because of his major part in the decision on the acceptability of the available solutions or outcomes as they emerge during the course of the negotiation. There are many possible definitions of negotiation, but the core is that it is a means adopted for the resolution of a conflict of interest. The conflict may be real, that is objective, or purely subjective. In the latter case, analysis or enlightened self-interest would show that there is little or nothing between the parties. The means adopted is an interchange of communication. The relationship between the process and the outcome of negotiation is incapable of being charted. It is not even certain what the skills are which are involved in negotiation. Some qualities such as sensitivity, responsiveness, keenness of intuition seem necessary components of such skills. But then an excess of such qualities, which might be styled over-sensitivity, susceptibility and proneness to gut reaction, would probably be disabilities. It is far from established that negotiating skills can be taught, rather than developed by experience.

Negotiation by lawyers

Some American universities study techniques of negotiation. The social psychology of negotiation also is a possible though not necessarily rewarding field of study.[3] Our focus, though, is neither on techniques nor psychology, but on the impact of professional ethics on the process of negotiation. In what ways does the adversarial system, within whose framework lawyers operate, determine the format and type of negotiations, in which lawyers ought to join and how they should conduct them?

In a negotiating team

Lawyers may negotiate as members of an *ad hoc* professional team, which covers the relevant range of expertise. The lawyer may not necessarily be the team leader. In a company take-over, this is usually the merchant banker who uses the other members as specialist advisers. Sometimes the lawyer's part in the negotiation shrinks to little more than a watching brief. He may have to stay sufficiently awake during long interchanges in alien terminology on building construction, or the application of accounting standards to depreciation and the like, to be able to observe or intervene when the argument touches a tangential point of law. He may be there in an entirely or nearly passive role just because he is the client's professional confidant, his most trusted adviser. The lawyer should be wary of crossing boundaries into the territory of another member's expertise, particularly when it is someone on his own side. If he is right, it will be resented. If he is wrong

---

3 Cf. 'Psychology of the Negotiator' by A I Phillips in the Conveyancing Review, Vol I, No 5, p 149, in which negotiation is broken down into persuasion, suggestion and manipulation, and I W Zartman *The 50% Solution* (Doubleday Anchor, 1976) pp 483–4: 'Theory about negotiation still not well developed, either in abstract terms or a fortiori in terms that can be used to explain real outcomes'.

he dents his reputation for the qualities of wisdom, balance, soundness, *gravitas* or whatever, which the good lawyer is supposed to bring to the negotiating table. Either way, he is liable to excite retaliation from, typically, the accountant, in the breast of many of whom is a barrack-room lawyer just dying for a chance to get out.

Negotiations with the client's opponent

The barrier to communication by a lawyer with the lawyer's client on the other side extends, of course, to direct negotiations with him. But there is nothing against negotiation between a lawyer, with his client alongside or not, and an unrepresented party, provided that the party has knowingly placed himself in that position. Such a situation, though, hobbles the lawyer in at least three ways. Most broadly, the professional protectiveness which the lawyer must extend not only to his own client but, whenever appropriate, beyond him to other lay persons, means that the lawyer should not seek advantage from one-sided legal arguments. If the negotiation results in agreement, the enforceability of any deed prepared by the lawyer there and then and signed by the parties is quite uncertain. If the agreement is not put into writing, second thoughts in the cooling-off period may supervene to fudge the terms or lead to reintroduction of the opponent client's lawyer who was originally unwanted. In the face of *ex post facto* recantation along the lines of 'my lawyer won't let me do it', the (unspoken) retort 'why didn't you bring him in in the first place' provides little comfort.

Client's presence at negotiations

The lawyers may negotiate, each flanked by his client, or by themselves. The presence of the client has the advantage/ disadvantage that instructions are immediately available, point by point as they arise, and an agreement can be clinched by the terminal handshake. Why might this be a disadvantage? Clients, seduced by the surface bond which often characterises the negotiation table, are prone to make concessions where they ought to take a stand. Conversely, they may bargain when they ought to concede. They may destroy an argument by contradicting its premise through failure to grasp its logic. In general terms, what is lost is the chance for consultation outside the hurly-burly – consultation, that valuable process where the adviser and his client stand back to assess the position in a partisan way.

Negotiation on values

Good lawyers are generally considered to be good negotiators. Some lawyers are highly experienced in negotiation. The lawyer ought not to negotiate, however, outwith the range of his professional expertise. In particular, he should not engage on his own in negotiations which turn on values fixed by a market or based on comparables. Unless he takes advice on the market or is helped to assess the comparables by the appropriate expert, he runs the risk of falling below the standard of competence. If he does, he commits a breach of professional ethics. Contradictorily, it is usually a lawyer who negotiates the amount of compensation in a reparation case, even though his counterpart is often not another lawyer, but an insurance company assessor. That practice is justifiable, since the tariff on which quantification is based, the valuation of claims, depends on estimations by judges in comparable cases. The lawyer can, therefore, approach this type of negotiation with a well-informed and rational perspective.

Horse-trading

Not so haggling, in its more sophisticated but still primitive version, bargaining or horse-trading, where it is the client, not the lawyer, who must decide whether the horse offered is the one he wants. These entail powerplays, position-taking and snap decisions, all of which are the client's prerogative. A powerplay is a threat to exploit an extraneous strength of the client's situation to force a concession which the other side has not been persuaded to give. Legitimate powerplays are the setting of time-limits, feet-dragging when the other side must

hurry, signalling the impending breakdown of the negotiation, allowing a stage of the negotiations to break down,
flaunting the alternative course open to the client – playing
hard to get – demonstrating commitment to the negotiations
– there is no alternative – putting on the frighteners, pleading
for mercy. It will be seen that each of these powerplays can
be used as a counter to another. They are risky tactics. It is in
many cases unethical for the lawyer to initiate a powerplay or
a counterplay or a response to either. If he does, he may be
usurping the client's prerogative. It is for the client to take the
decisions; it is for the client to take the risks; it is for the client
to choose from among legitimate tactics; it is for the client to
determine for himself how much and what sort of pressure to
put on the other side.

Reconciliation of positions

Where the lawyer comes into his own is in principled
negotiation with a strong professional adversary. The point
of negotiation is to explore the relative strengths of the
opening positions. The best possible outcome of a negotiation is the reconciliation of those positions. Their apparent
opposition comes from zero-sum thinking. (This notion
was, so far as we know, first conceived by Ralf Dahrendorf.)
This has as its underlying assumption the preconceived idea
that to the extent of your gain I suffer an exactly equal detriment. It is the arithmetic of envy. For example in a commercial lease, I the tenant want to minimise my expenditure; one
way to do that is to pay a lower insurance premium, which I
can achieve by limiting the insured risks; zero-sum thinking
leads me to believe that a higher insurance premium is a gain
for you the landlord and an equal loss for me. If the landlord's solicitor is a strong negotiator, he will point out the
fallacy. The landlord gains nothing from the payment of a
higher premium. But the tenant will lose from a reduction of
the premium by a cutback in the range of insured risks. The
reason is that, under the lease, the exception from the tenant's
repairing liability will be limited to damage caused by an
insured risk.

Litigation to be avoided, if possible

The purpose of negotiation is to resolve a dispute or disagreement represented by a gap between the positions. If the gap arises from a genuine difference in principle, it will not necessarily be a good strategy for the lawyer-negotiator to attempt to beat down the other side so that the other client's interest receives utterly no vindication. Such an outcome is offensive to the sense of fairness. The strategy raises the temperature and so pushes one of the parties in the direction of litigation. As has been said (p 83), it is against professional ethics for a lawyer to stir up litigation.

Counsel's opinion in negotiations

The lawyer-negotiator should be reasonably certain as to both the law and the facts underlying his argument. Another way of putting it is that only good faith arguments should be advanced. An interesting and amusing illustration is the use of counsel's opinion in this area. For one reason or another, counsel's opinion does not appear, as often nowadays as formerly, as a counter in negotiation. It takes too long to obtain; it is designed to be balanced as between the contrary viewpoints; in certain areas at least, the solicitor's analysis of the law should be equivalent to counsel's analysis; the appropriate stage for counsel's opinion is when the negotiations have already broken down and the chances of success in litigation fall to be explored. If 'eminent' counsel's opinion is brandished, so to speak, in negotiations, with the claim that it is totally supportive of one side, the other side's lawyer should ask to see it. It is wrong, where it is preventable, to allow a party to persist in futile negotiations. A refusal to disclose the opinion probably means that it is fence-sitting, as it normally is. Misrepresentation of counsel's opinion is not a good faith argument.

Virtuous compromise

If the interests cannot be reconciled, a compromise should be sought. A good solicitor is creative not only in finding partisan arguments, but also in searching out compromises which leave his client with somewhat more of an advantage than is called for by the merits. Perhaps the true mission of the solicitor is to find persuasive compromises. Apart from all the other well-recognised drawbacks of litigation, its major failure is that it is bound to come up with an all-or-nothing result.

Second negotiation

Unless the client is present and the lawyer and he negotiate in unison, or the negotiation's outcome is within the scope of the lawyer-negotiator's mandate, the lawyer's position must be understood to be reserved pending instructions from the client. This may well involve a second negotiation, this time between lawyer and client. We have said that inherent in negotiation is a conflict of interest. If the parties' interests are reconciled, then the negotiation resolves itself purely into a discussion on further procedure. When the lawyer is said to 'negotiate' with his client, wherein then lies the conflict of interest? After all, we have claimed as the ethical starting-point the identification of the lawyer's interest with the client's interest. The conflict of interest, after the first negotiation, which necessitates the second, is simply the discrepancy between the lawyer's revised (revised, that is, in the light of the discussions at the negotiating table) perception of the client's interest and the client's unaltered version.

Lawyer's interest

It is accurate to say that the lawyer now has an interest, that is a personal investment, in the conclusion reached in the negotiation, unless he is reporting to the client that his argument has held complete sway or that the negotiation has failed. A negotiation fails when the other side's closing position gives less to his client than the lawyer reasonably believes can be achieved by other means. In the second negotiation, the lawyer seeks to persuade his client to see it his way. That way follows the lines of the consensus reached at the first negotiation. Professional ethics dictates that yet again it is the client's perception of his interest which must in the end prevail. Exceptionally, the application of this principle may lead the lawyer to withdraw from the agency. One such case is where the outcome of the negotiation falls clearly within the range of the lawyer's mandate from the client, so enabling the lawyer to enter into a commitment, legally binding or not, at the conclusion of the meeting; if the client subsequently repudiates the mandate the lawyer may decide that he should no longer act. More contentiously, the lawyer may withdraw if the action insisted on by the client, even in the face of the other side's arguments and disclosures in the course of the negotiation, is morally repugnant to the lawyer. An example would be where the lawyer considered such action to be oppressive. In the first example, the client has destroyed the mutual confidence at the core of the professional relationship. In the second, the lawyer resiles from pursuit of what he believes to be an unworthy cause. Such a stand runs counter to the concept of the lawyer as a 'hired gun'. In either case, there has to be adherence to the general principle that the lawyer should terminate the relationship only if or when no damage will be caused to the client's interest.

Lawyer's proper stance in negotiations

One can see that the lawyer should not too heavily invest in the conclusions of the negotiation in the knowledge that his interest must yield to the client's. Even if he goes no further than a promise to 'recommend' them, he suffers two weaknesses if the recommendation is rejected. Not only has he failed to represent, but he has also inaccurately assessed, the strength which the client considers to attach to his position. This delimitation of the lawyer's proper stance is just an instance of the principle that the lawyer should maintain a low profile. That principle has application too in the lawyer's manner of negotiation. He cannot help it if he happens to be a charismatic negotiator, that is, one whose utterances, no matter how banal, unaccountably silence the room. There is, anyway, no direct relationship between charisma and success in negotiation. Nor should the lawyer-negotiator, although his methods ought primarily to be based on persuasion by reasoned argument, shun completely the employment of suggestion or manipulation. Outside of mathematics, with its passionless xs and ys, there is no such thing as pure reason. What he has to avoid or, being only human, minimise is *personal* investment in display. He is not there to score points.

Reduction to writing

Parties enter negotiations with the expectation, at least the hope, or at the very least the pretence, that they are the road to agreement. Agreements of importance should be reduced to writing by lawyers. The justification for that proposition lies in the irony implicit in the word 'reduce'. In the case of the commercial lease, the reality is that half a page or so of agreed terms is 'reduced' to a document of upwards of 50 pages; a company acquisition consisting of a single-sentence agreement to purchase the capital of X Limited at the price of £y per share will be 'reduced' to a document of at least the same size. What is the relationship between the curt agreement and the prolix agreement?

Mega-missives

House purchase is an interesting case. An agreement on price and entry used to be converted into a one-page offer with a handful of clauses, responded to by an unqualified acceptance. Nowadays, exactly the same agreement is 'reduced' to an interchange of formal letters aptly nicknamed mega-missives. Despite the tendency to standardisation on both the purchaser's and the vendor's side, mega-missives have the disadvantage that they introduce contentious points. Where before there was agreement, now there is ample room for disagreement. Are the purchaser's solicitors' proposals, which assume an opening position he will readily give up, conceived in the true interest of his client? Are mega-missives ethical in that the client is not in most cases given the chance to choose between the greater probability of conclusion of a binding bargain if the terms are neutral and, on the other side, the possibility that the other party may agree to provisions angled in the offeror's favour?

Fair balance

The counter-balance has to be that the solicitor's purpose is no more than to protect his client's interest. But is that, though, the client's interest, as the client, avid for a commitment, would perceive it? Is it not the case that the lawyer has some subtle personal interest, a quiet investment in the effectiveness and comprehensiveness of his 'house-style' of offer for the purchase of a house? By this stage of the game, most solicitors about to offer for a house have played the counterpart roles of purchaser's and seller's agent often enough to know what provisions in missives strike a fair balance between both.

Negotiation by correspondence

In the process of 'reduction' to writing, of documentation, the lawyer faces the same problems as in negotiation, but in a worse form. The draftsman and the reviser engage in negotiation, so to speak, in the form of correspondence, which may be finalised by a face-to-face meeting to close the gaps. Since the documentary process is phased over the stages of revisal, counter-revisal, sometimes counter-counter-revisal and final adjustment, the type of secondary negotiation between solicitor and client, which we mentioned above, to align reasonably acceptable compromise wording with the client's view may take place more than once. The two differences from face-to-face negotiation here, are that there is already a basic agreement between the parties and, in the second place, the pros and cons of the issues are for the client much less intellectually accessible. Professional ethics again sets limits on partisanship. One lawyer should not take advantage of clerical error or incompetence on the other's part. Put another way, the document should reflect the basic agreement. If the solicitor inadvertently adds a 0 to the purchase price, the other should not rush in and accept it. More plausibly, if the deal is a purchase of a business as a going concern, the purchaser's lawyer should not grab at a document which leaves the liabilities with the vendor unless such an arrangement is part of the basic agreement.

Ethics of draftsmanship

Beyond the confines of the basic agreement, the terms of which ought, as we have said, to be faithfully reproduced in the documents, what sets the objectives of the parties' lawyers? What we are asking for, in other words, are the ethics of draftsmanship and revisalmanship[4]. In relation to megamissives for the sale and purchase of residential property, we suggested above that the ethical path lay in the direction of the adoption by both sides of non-aligned provisions, a reasonable working definition of those being fair terms as between seller and purchaser. This may come to pass for reasons which will emerge from an analysis of the development of the commercial lease.

Leonine lease

In the early days of commercial leasing in Scotland, the tendency was for the formal document to be made up of three distinguishable parts. There were the main terms, rent, duration, rent review cycle and so on, which had been agreed before the transaction reached the solicitors. There was a group of subordinate points, restrictions on alienation, automatic uplift in rent on subletting, joint and several obligations on the original tenant and those succeeding by assignation, disregard for rent review purposes of tight constraint on use, none of which had been agreed but which were introduced by the draftsman at the behest of the landlord. Insofar as these struck at the marketability of the tenant's interest, so lowering

---

4 As to revisalmanship see a series of articles by A I Phillips in the Conveyancing Review: Revisalmanship I, Vol I, May 1959, p 229; Revisalmanship II, Vol I, August 1959, p 266; Revisalmanship III, Vol II, November 1959, p 19; Revisalmanship IV, Vol II, February 1960, p 55; Revisalmanship V, Vol II, May 1960, p 92; Revisalmanship Concluded, Vol II, August 1960, p 123.

its market value, they constituted unfair terms. Despite that, they were often swallowed whole for reasons which do not concern us here. The point for us is that the landlord's opening position, as expressed in the pristine terms of the draft, although harsh, corresponded to the landlord's perception of his interest. Thus, there was nothing ethically wrong with the production of what was a leonine draft by the landlord's solicitor. Apart from the main terms and the subordinate points, the rest of the document was standardised.

Advent of the hyperlease

Market factors and greater professional sophistication have wrought great changes in this simple scene. In place of a harsh draft, which had often come back unscathed from the other side, a much more reasonable opening version was now likely to initiate protracted to-and-fro negotiations between draftsman and reviser engulfing even those terms which had previously been standard. The document inexorably grew longer in the process. Historically, the hyperlease preceded the mega-missives.

Hyperlease game

Although the hyperlease was, with the benefit of the reviser's contributions, a much more highly-developed product than its simple predecessor, the stances of both the draftsman and the reviser were often ethically dubious. Through specialised experience with many varieties of the hyperlease, conveyancers gained insight into how the individual clauses interacted and how shifts of meaning could be subtly achieved by small changes in wording and even manipulation of punctuation. The adjustment of commercial leases came to resemble games of chess. The draftsman's opening gambit was met by the reviser's favourite defence, designed to cause disarray throughout the hostile position. Conveyancers boasted of the x number of traps and pitfalls for the unwary hidden in their styles of draft or their standard revisals. Not only that, but the finer and the not so fine points of the game went far beyond the understanding of many of the clients, on whose behalf the contests were ostensibly being fought and who were supposed to be directing the moves. The lawyers had taken over and were having intellectual fun.

Setting traps

It is obvious from what has been said that in so doing conveyancers went over the top from the standpoint of professional ethics. To set traps is to treat the other lawyer as a *personal* adversary, which is directly contrary to the working principles of the adversarial system. For the lawyer to outrun the client's understanding of the issues is to uncouple himself from the client's interest, as defined for the purposes of professional ethics, which he has a responsibility to pursue. Of course there were casualties. Landlords lost attractive tenants, and tenants attractive premises, because of misunderstood, half-understood, or not at all understood, positions taken up by their lawyers.

Postmodern hyperlease

The hyperlease has now moved, or perhaps is now moving, into a new phase. The adversarial energies which have stimulated and shaped its development, have been the landlord's requirement for complete, unfettered and explicit[5] controls over the tenant's use and occupation of the premises and, on the other side, the tenant's interest in freedom. There have been changes in philosophy emerging from the solicitors' battles of the previous phase. Where the landlord then saw his interest as lying in arbitrary powers, possessed of which he could be judge in his own cause, he is now prone to accept the objectivity of the principles of good estate management. Where he felt before that it was a good idea to rid himself of

---

5 The notion that the answer to every contingency which might affect the landlord-tenant relationship should be capable of being read off the lease is the factor mainly responsible for its growth in length.

management chores by, for example, laying the obligation on the tenant to maintain the insurance and re-instate damage caused by an insured risk, he now, himself, undertakes these obligations. The criterion of fairness is beginning to creep by way of judicial interpretation into the connotation of the reasonable landlord. What might be called the postmodern hyperlease has still some way to go. If commercial lawyers will drop, even more than they have already done, zero-sum thinking (see p 97) in favour of a more strictly ethical approach, its progress will be accelerated.

Summing-up

Where we have just ended up with our analysis of the lawyer's stewardship of the commercial lease makes a good jumping-off point from which to sum up the impact of the adversarial framework on the ethical dimension of the lawyer-client relationship. A potted version of the conclusion was that the solicitor has a duty to be partisan, but at the same time he is ethically more comfortable with a position which fairly accommodates the other side's interest and is broadly in line with ordinary morality. There will be tension then between the client's interest, as originally conceived by an aggressive or unscrupulous client, and the solicitor's perception of what it ought to be. In most cases, the influence of the solicitor is exerted in the direction of moderation, but sometimes he considers it right to suggest a stiffening of the client's resolve. If seen through a distorting lens, this intermediation by the lawyer may appear as half-heartedness unworthy of a citizen's champion or, the other way, as an irritant stinging the client in the direction of insecurity. Society or the public interest exhibits a parallel conflict. One concern is with open access to justice. The other lies in the resolution of disputes short of litigation. The pre-conditions for the reconciliation of these conflicting societal concerns have already been demonstrated. In the first place, a system of justice must be adversarial. The individual's grievance must be focused on an adversary. A grievance against society at large, or the world, or the gods, is – sometimes sadly in the first case, but rightly in the other cases where it amounts to a refusal to accept ill-luck – just non-justiciable. The system starts at the solicitor's door and ends in the House of Lords. In between, the course taken by an individual dispute or transaction depends much more than is realised on the system of professional ethics conceived by lawyers and their standards of adherence to it.

Chapter 5

Standing

Professional etiquette

What has become of professional etiquette? It figures in the first edition (1976) of *The Websters*[1], but had vanished by the second edition (1984). It received a mention in *The Professional Conduct and Etiquette of Solicitors* (The Law Society, 1960) by Sir Thomas Lund CBE in his scheme, which distinguished 'three grades of improper professional conduct', the distinctions, he pointed out, being fine ones: professional misconduct, unprofessional conduct and breach of etiquette. These categories would now be obsolete in disciplinary proceedings in view of the approach of the tribunal and the courts to misconduct; cf. p 12. Before its disappearance, professional etiquette used to be defined as professional good manners. Have the good manners disappeared along with the vocabulary?

Etiquette

'What is etiquette', a child asks his mother in a recent TV commercial for Heinz soup. The boy had been eating his soup in the wrong way—spooning inwards instead of outwards. The mother explained to the child with some hesitation, as if searching in her memory for some half-forgotten concept,

---

1 *The Websters*: 'if you lose your reputation . . . you will . . . harm the whole profession'; IBA's International Code of Ethics: 'Lawyers shall at all times . . . abstain from any behaviour which may tend to discredit the profession of which they are members'; CCBE Code: 'Relationships of trust can only exist if a lawyer's personal honour, honesty and integrity are beyond doubt. For the lawyer these traditional virtues are professional obligations'.

that 'etiquette' was a French word and meant 'good manners'. The whole family were then shown, every member of it eating soup the wrong way – but with gusto. The point had been made that etiquette was something foreign, belonging to the past, which got in the way of wholehearted enjoyment of life. Etiquette had been wiped away in the space of a TV commercial.

Etiquette and ethics

In what seems perhaps a doomed rearguard action, Professor Robert Mohan has defined civility as 'the outer ramparts of morality'. If the ramparts are crumbling, is the fortress of morality itself about to be razed to the ground? Put it another way, if etiquette has drowned in the soup of commercialism is morality not already gasping for breath? (Significantly, lifebelts are being thrown: see Chapter 6 at p 145.)

Etiquette rests on convention

Etiquette was, as we saw, Lund's lowest grade of standardised professional conduct. Undoubtedly, etiquette consists of low-level rules for acceptable social behaviour. If the boy in the commercial, instead of launching his fundamental attack on the very conception of etiquette by questioning its lexical existence, had asked his mother to justify the well-mannered way of eating soup, she would have been hard pressed for an answer. The modes of etiquette rest purely on convention, they are accepted ways of doing things. If the child, refusing to accept convention as justification, persisted with his questioning, the mother, if she did not choose to concede, would have had to fall back on authority, *her* authority. The child would be ordered away from the table or out of the room if his defiance continued. (Admittedly, this scenario has much less verisimilitude nowadays than the Heinz commercial, but it makes a useful paradigm, as will be seen later.)

Etiquette rooted in group

Outsiders may deviate from rules of etiquette without incurring disapproval, although disapproval by members of one religious or ethnic group of behaviour which deviates from their rules of etiquette, by members of another such group is, rightly, criticised as racist. But in places held sacred, the non-believer is expected to conform (in churches, all present should be bare-headed; in synagogues, all should have their heads covered.) There, etiquette is overlaid with sanctification of the rules. The sanction for frequent or outrageous (evoking outrage rather than mere disapproval) contravention of a rule of etiquette is expulsion from the group or, less formally, ostracism. (If we go back to the mother and child, the less formal sanction, instead of dismissal from the room, corresponding to expulsion from the group, would be aversion of the maternal gaze. The mildest response is 'tut-tutting', the equivalent of admonishing.) It is evident then that the rules of etiquette are rooted in the group.

Etiquette in sub-groups

Nowadays, society has diversified into many sub-groups, with distinctive sub-cultures, much of whose vitality lies in what can be regarded as peculiar forms of etiquette. At the time of writing, punk comes to mind as an example. The authority from whom the binding force of etiquette derives is the head, as in the family, or the self-constituted or elected leader, or in marxian theory, the ruling class. Where the source of the binding force is *absolute* authority, breach of etiquette may mean a sentence of death. (Pu Yi, the last Manchu emperor, a 'sanitinised' version of whom was the subject of a recent Oscar-winning film, was said to have the power to inflict cruel punishments, even death, on members of his retinue who transgressed etiquette; cf. Queen of Hearts' way with capital punishment – 'Off with their heads!' – in Alice in Wonderland.) Where groupings are in a phase of rapid transformation, breaking up and re-forming, as in teenage groups in the last few decades, rules of etiquette show patterns which are both unstable and, contradictorily, iconic (that is, having semi-sacred qualities so that breach is regarded as disgraceful and amounting to serious misconduct; cf. definition of professional misconduct p 12).

Etiquette based on sheer tradition seems now to be steadily weakening, while the iconic etiquette of sub-groups ramifies and renews itself over and over again. There is an even newer phenomenon, which might be called 'designer etiquette'. Novel life-styles are picked up from the media consisting almost entirely of outward trappings and mannerisms, the stuff of etiquette. There is an iconic element also in designer etiquette. What is shared, what holds the members of the particular sub-group together, is the cult of an 'idol'. Those who hold to traditional etiquette become outdated. If asked to explain or justify themselves, like the mother by the boy in the soup commercial, they cannot. In a sub-culture, its rules of etiquette not only work positively to create solidarity, but also negatively to defy traditional etiquette. Conformity to etiquette is both a mark of membership and a condition of membership as well.

Some illustrations

Before we apply these ideas to professional etiquette, it will be useful to try them out in some hypothetical situations.

Exclusive restaurant

At one table in a 'select' or 'exclusive' restaurant, a man removes his jacket and tie. The manager asks him and his party to leave. The description applied to the restaurant shows that it is 'selective' in whom it admits and whom it excludes. Approved diners will be members of a group which understands and is prepared to conform to the rule of etiquette which decrees that a jacket and tie will be worn by men when dining. Those prepared to conform to that rule can reasonably be expected to follow other similar rules of etiquette.

Flashers and streakers

This is, although it need not be, a masculine preserve. Female 'streakers' are not, so far as we know, charged. Why is there sexual discrimination in this respect and what is the reason for the comparatively severe punishment inflicted on the flasher? He represents a threat to the sexual mores of his society. To deviate as he has done, in the teeth of powerful conventions, is taken as an indication of a dangerous potentiality for even more harmful types of sexual deviance. The aggression which underlies such an act is also an important factor in the determination of the punishment.

Shirtless six

A few years ago on a sunny day in New York, six women met in Central Park and proceeded in unison to strip to the waist. They had given ample advance notice of their intention, so a crowd had gathered to watch. They were led away by the police and charged with breach of the peace. Their act was intended to be symbolic. It represented an assertion of feminist rights. Since there were topless men sunning themselves in the park, true equality entitled women to do the same. The women's intention was to pursue their point of constitutional principle as far as the Supreme Court.

Analysis

Only the first case was a breach of etiquette; the second was immoral (we are not concerned here with its criminality) and amounted to a breach of ethics; the third was neither. The first two represented a threat to the shared values of the relevant group, in the second case society as a whole. Streaking was regarded as an eccentricity. If we assume that the restaurant in the first illustration represents the society of lawyers (if for lawyers we read solicitors, this would be co-extensive with the membership of the Law Society), the removal of the jacket and tie would correspond to a breach of professional etiquette.

Professional etiquette for lawyers

When reliance on tradition and authority for justification of rules of any sort is seen to be unprincipled, as tends to be the case now, the true foundation of etiquette as emblematic of group membership becomes clear. When the newly-admitted advocate acquires his wig, when the purchaser's solicitor attends on the seller's solicitor for the settlement, when the lawyer wore his bowler hat to and from his office or chambers, when the solicitor-pleader calls the opposing advocate his 'learned friend', when the solicitor journeys to consult the advocate, when the new trainee dons a (unisex) suit for his or her first day in the office – all these are signifiers of adherence to the relevant professional group. Three in the list are odd men out: few lawyers now wear bowler hats; advocates now sometimes call on solicitors; slaves to time as they have become, solicitors now settle most transactions by post or despatch-rider. To say then that professional etiquette for lawyers has weakened is less accurate than to say that it has been reduced in scope. Much of the paraphernalia of etiquette remains: wigs, gowns, modes of address, court decorum.

If the justification for rules of etiquette is that they demonstrate solidarity, they will be endowed with ethical or quasi-ethical binding force only if, and to the extent that, demonstrations of allegiance or continued allegiance to the group have themselves such force. Breaches of etiquette are reasonably taken to represent a general threat to play fast and loose with rules of a higher order. In other words, flouting of professional etiquette is felt – whether empirically justified or not – to reveal a propensity to defy professional ethics.

Etiquette as formality

The legal profession, above all others, emphasises professional etiquette and is often publicly criticised for it. Is there a good reason for the emphasis and so a good defence against the criticism? Etiquette used sometimes to be called 'good form'. Law and the legal system are permeated with formalities, that is, matters of form (see discussion in *The Lawyer and Society* p 102 *et seq* on Solemnity). But the direction in which they evolve is away from formality. Roman law matured from formal to consensual contracts. Probative writing becomes less a form essential for the constitution of certain agreements and more the requisite mode of proof. The narrowing in the range of the rules of professional etiquette, to which we have drawn attention, is a movement in the same direction. Acts with strong legal force, such as dispositions, leases, wills, summonses are still serious matters, which deserve to be performed after due deliberation and should demonstrate their gravity by conformity to established solemn procedures. Such demonstrations are directed implicitly to whom they may concern (formerly, wills and powers of attorney were *expressly* so directed). In the same way, the forms of professional etiquette have significance for, are picked up as demonstrations by, members of the public as well as by members of the profession. As with all signifiers, they form a system of their own.

Image with a quill pen

What characterises that system in the lawyers' case? Since so many of the rules of professional etiquette for lawyers involve long-established modes, mannerisms and procedures, the image of the lawyer which is built up by and for the public out of the mental collage of such elements is of an antiquated practitioner going about his traditional affairs in the time-honoured ways. While the real solicitor's mental functioning has accelerated to keep up with his laser printer, his representation in the public image stubbornly continues to write with a quill pen.

Ill-fitting image

Even though the lineaments of the lawyer's public image have proved in recent times to be so at odds with, so impervious to the realities, lawyers remain anxious about the profession's public relations, about the appearances which it presents to society. An ill-effect – perhaps the most important – of some breaches of professional etiquette is conceived to be the undesirable impression which may thus be conveyed to the public.

Serious breach of this sort may be treated as misconduct. The irony is that, in view of the misfit between the stuffiness of the lawyer's image and his real features, it can easily be that the 'unprofessional' lawyer, instead of sullying the image, acquires in the eyes of the public something like a folk-heroic, swashbuckling reputation.

Professional etiquette and aggression

In a previous paragraph, we found the binding force of etiquette to originate in the sense of solidarity which comes from membership of a particular group. Its rules were like the rules of a club. As yet, though, no clue has emerged as to what features of a particular rule qualify it to be a rule of professional etiquette for lawyers. For example, the instruction that every guest must be signed in by a club member would hardly be thought of as a rule of etiquette for a private club. What we want now to suggest is that the special character of the rules of professional etiquette, that which gives them their distinctiveness, is derived from the adversarial system within which lawyers work (see previous chapter for the argument that adversarial relationships are pervasive throughout the legal process). Lord Diplock described the court process as 'bloodless fisticuffs'. Professional etiquette is designed, although perhaps not consciously, to maintain and at the same time to demonstrate the bloodlessness of the fisticuffs. Mannered modes of address, polite exchanges, banter with no more than the right degree of bite, drain away the aggression from forensic encounters. The pecking order among judges, senior advocates, juniors, solicitors measures out the doses of aggression which can safely be used by one against another.

Etiquette and the gentleman

To release aggression in the midst of a social encounter in what was formerly called 'polite society' was judged to be crude, rough, ungentlemanly. So some of the attributes of gentlemanliness, irrelevant as they might be, were appropriated as ingredients of the rules of professional etiquette.

The ideal of the gentleman has decayed in our times, at least so far as those outward manifestations, which the person of today would dismiss as empty manners, are concerned. (The feminist attack on the concept of the 'lady' has had an influence.) That probably accounts for the abandonment of those rules of professional etiquette which have been dropped. (The cars belonging to advocates parked outside Parliament House used always to be of 'gentlemanly' makes – nothing flashy. Edinburgh and Glasgow used to manifest, to the connoisseur of such things at least, subtly differentiated styles of etiquette, in relation to which Edinburgh asserted an unstated superiority while Glasgow was aggressively defensive. Now they are at, or approaching, the point of interchangeability. Law firms long established in Glasgow are opening offices in Edinburgh and vice versa.) The less professional etiquette smacks of gentlemanliness and the more it stands as a means for the control of aggression, the less its rules resemble the rules of a club, the more they are like the rules of a game (cf. Chapter 4 at p 80).

Appearance

Etiquette is designed to present a particular appearance. As we have said, behaviour which is obedient to etiquette is both a condition and a sign of membership. The sign is intended to be read and understood just as much by outsiders as by other members, if not more so. The principal features which the lawyers' professional etiquette is designed to present are, as we have seen, *gravitas* (high seriousness), a modern version of gentlemanliness and control of aggression. Add perhaps adherence to tradition. The lawyer whose behaviour breaks with a rule of etiquette in a way which *appears* to defy it parallels the case of the 'misbehaving' man in the restaurant in the first illustration. He incurs disapproval. He is seen as unworthy of membership, that is, of the status analogous to that of the *habitue* of a select restaurant. His behaviour is a threat to the way in which the profession wants to present itself. It may damage the reputation of the profession. It is for that reason that the lawyer's departure from etiquette is unethical.

Moral lapses

Even if we ignore its criminality, the conduct of the man in the second illustration is of a kind which does not allow us to find a parallel within the scope of professional etiquette. Nevertheless, if a lawyer was discovered to have been guilty of indecent exposure or something of comparable gravity, we would want to class his behaviour as a breach of professional ethics. He would not have failed in whole-hearted pursuit of his client's interest; nor would his conduct fly in the face of some universal value – the attitudes of different societies to nakedness show no consistency; he would not have infringed the rules of the adversarial system; nor, as we have already said, does an offence of this type lie inside the range of professional etiquette. Significantly, our impulsion to stigmatise such an act as professionally unethical accords with generally accepted principle. Some moral lapses then, amount to professionally unethical behaviour in the same way as do breaches of professional etiquette.

Integrity

It would seem then that we should add the quality or qualities designated by integrity to the shortlist of those which the legal profession seeks to cultivate in its corporate character. What saved the Shirtless Six in our third illustration from charges of breach of etiquette or ethics was integrity. They were defying convention for the sake of principle. People might think that the principle was wrong or silly, but such a view on the part of others would not detract from the women's integrity. In the lawyer's case, the client's interest may lead him to confront authority or convention or even oppose the side of virtue or equity, but that constitutes a test, not a denial, of his integrity. If, though, one were to come to the conclusion that the women's act was not truly in pursuit of principle but that it was actuated by some form of exhibitionism, a different construction would be put on their action. What is important in this context is the *appearance* of integrity.

Grassing

What we have brought out so far is that the lawyer has an ethical responsibility for the corporate character of the profession. He has a duty to manifest the 'select' qualities in his behaviour in and out of the office. What if he comes across a serious case of ethical backsliding in a colleague? An article by Laurie Taylor in *Observer Magazine* of 15 January 1989 starts off:

> 'Few sights are more intimidating than a pack of moralists in pursuit of an admission of guilt.'

Underlying this is the common feeling that, although personal morality is admirable, to impose morality on others, or even to engage in armtwisting to force them to accept blame, is somehow priggish, sanctimonious. In the course of his article, Professor Taylor comments that among the professional criminals he had met for the purpose of his study, the only activity which aroused guilt was 'informing, grassing, on their mates'. Middle managers at a seminar to sample a new training exercise in London were confronted by a similar problem (this was reported in an article in the *Financial Times* on 1 June 1989). They were supposed, in searching a colleague's desk for some data, to have come across a huge backlog of work. They had to choose between three options: report the find to their joint boss; say nothing; or mention the matter to the colleague privately and ask if they could be of help. One group unanimously picked the option of a quiet chat and offer of help. The other group all agreed that they would rat on their colleague to the boss. It transpired that the second group were all members of an organisation whose ethos demanded total commitment from each employee to his task. But the first group approached the exercise as if they were designing an organisation in which all employees would find it rewarding to work. If we transpose the same circumstances into the environment of legal practice, we meet a similar conflict of values. On the one hand, there is loyalty to a colleague. On the other, not only is there the profession's commitment to its client but also its concern with its corporate character.

Evaluation of corporate character

The manner in which other people evaluate in terms of their own experience one's characteristic tendencies to act and respond in particular ways can be said, from one point of view, to determine one's character (although from the psychological point of view, character would be defined in terms of the tendencies themselves). This is especially so with a social phenomenon such as corporate character. Lawyers, as we have suggested, seek to cultivate and maintain such characteristics as high seriousness, elements preserved from the tradition of the gentleman, control of aggression, adherence to tradition and integrity. People may perceive them, instead, as pompous, elitist, stodgy, over-conservative, inflexible. These are the same qualities, only differently evaluated.

Judgment by appearances

This appeared in an early draft of the American Lawyer's Code but was omitted from the published version:

> 'A lawyer shall avoid acting in such a way that a *fair-minded* person, knowing all of the relevant facts that are readily available, would conclude that, in the generality of such cases, disciplinary violations are likely to occur in a significant number of instances.' (author's italics)

The closing words indicate generalisation, that the rule is intended to relate to behaviour which is *significant* for a judgment of corporate character. Apart from that, the interesting reference is to the state of mind and knowledge of the person who is deemed to make the judgment. He should be fair and reasonably knowledgable but would undertake no research. This admirably defines the viewpoint from which an ethical evaluation of the lawyer's conduct *should* be made.

Image

Sadly, the social representation, evocatively called 'image', of the legal profession's corporate character, which is the most influential factor in the public perception of the lawyer is not composed from such a viewpoint. (The other main factor is, of course, clients' direct experience of lawyers, from which a totally different picture is formed; cf impressive statistics for client satisfaction in the most recent polls. Such 'hard facts' make no impact whatsoever on the lineaments of the image.) We mentioned above that the select characteristics projected corporately by lawyers might be viewed, so to speak, through a distorting lens with the result that they come to be differently evaluated by the public. It is the image which creates the distortion. The image-makers are the public relations industry. The media transmit the image to the public but they do more than passively transmit it. In many instances, pre-eminently in the case of the lawyer's image the features are established adversarially. For many years, the UK Law Societies have engaged in costly public relations campaigns, run by high-powered public relations committees, to try to eliminate or at least reduce the gap between the image and what they see as the reality, those select characteristics which are fostered by the profession. There cannot be many who would argue with the view that the exercise has been futile. (Some might try to say that, without the huge expenditure of time, money and effort, things might be worse. There is also a possible argument that they might have been better; cf. media reaction to English Bar's campaign against the Green Paper proposals below.)

Hostile government, consumers and press

The crunch came with the publication of the Green Papers produced by the government, standing for the public interest[2] backed by the consumer bodies, representing clients in general but failing to reflect the interests of individual clients (see statistics). In the media, the legal profession found itself totally friendless. Both the ideology of the Green Papers and the

---

2 But see this writer's radical criticisms of the provisions of the Green Paper for Scotland in (1988) 33 JLSS 234. In the writer's view the public interest was only partially (certainly not impartially) represented. The public interest in an independent legal profession was ignored.

virtually unanimous support by the media for their proposals (*The Times*, however, provided balanced coverage) fed largely on anti-lawyer sentiment. The opposition by senior and emeritus members of the English Bar was denounced as self-refuting, just because it was prompt and passionate. Some arguments in the press resembled a syllogism along the lines: the lawyers dislike the proposals/the public dislike lawyers/ therefore the proposals must be good. Significantly perhaps (see *ante*), the English Bar's highly-publicised[3] engagement of Saatchi and Saatchi to promote its opposition to the Green Paper at a reputed fee of £1m was itself used to undermine the campaign by the innuendo that it showed how poor the Bar's image must be. (In the same vein, this cry from the heart by a Soviet lawyer is worth reproducing, complete with the barbed comment, from the *Guardian* of 23 February 1989: 'He made the following declaration, which will doubtless qualify him for instant admission to the Lord Hailsham Hall of Fame for services to the self-image of lawyers everywhere "The services of advocates would be much more effective . . . if their prestige were not undermined by writers, journalists, and filmmakers . . . It would be difficult to recall a film or a newspaper feature where an advocate would figure as an intelligent and honest professional rather than a gabster pulling a criminal out of a sticky spot" ').

If public relations have failed, what then?

The public is aware of the conflict between the ethical dictates which shape the lawyer's professional responsibility and his commercial interest. The cynical and the profession's detractors suggest that the latter always prevails. This view emerges at three levels. In the first place, it is at the base of the concept of professionalism that the professional does for money what others do for nothing or for love (amateur is derived from *amare*: to love). Not only is prostitution supposed to be the

---

3 It was strange that the launching of the campaign by the Bar was so heavily publicised. Normally, public relations means relations with the public, conducted anything but publicly. Care is usually taken that the hand of public relations should remain invisible.

oldest form of professionalism, but it is also the one which fits that basic description most exactly. In its broader, derivative application, the term 'prostitution' is used to represent the stigma attached to the professional. He debases an art, a talent, a protective or caring relationship by commercialising it. The true artist starves in his garret. Nowadays, the money motive, greed, has become more respectable. The counterpart idea in professionalism that the professional is a serious, and, therefore, a more skilled, specialised performer is allowed to come to the fore. The competence of his performance contrasts with the amateurishness of the amateur.

Bound by precedent

The professional's downside is that he is not reputed to have flair, the quality which fosters creativity. Innovation is the preserve of the 'gifted amateur'. The lawyer, not just because he is professional, but in every other way, represents the very antithesis of the amateur as possessor of these high qualities. The epitome of the amateur in this sense is the writer or artist who pursues art for art's sake. Moliere chose the same analogy: 'writing is like prostitution, first you do it for the love of it, then you do it for a few friends and finally you do it for money'. This is how Kenneth Burke, sometimes described as an American sage, spoke about what he called the 'counterstatements' made by men of literature: 'Irony, novelty, experimentalism, vacillation, the cult of conflict. Are not these men trying to make us at home in indecision, are they not trying to humanise the state of doubt'? It is only too obvious that the 'statements' made by the lawyer are typical of those to be countered by such counterstatements. He represents literalness not 'irony', his language is aimed straight at precision, in his backward-looking search for precedent he shies away from novelty; he seeks safety so there is no indulgence in experimentalism; he gropes around for certainty pretending it is there when he knows it is not; he frets for a decision, any decision, but hoping for a fair or just one; every day he lives in conflict not to cultivate but to allay it; the law's order is claimed to be above all men, great or small.

High culture criticism

Austin Sarat (an American professor, in an article in *International Bar News* 1988 on the *Public Image of Lawyers*) identifies the tradition of what he calls 'high culture' criticism of lawyers. His 'favourite swipe', he says, is taken from Theodore Dreiser's novel *The Financier*:

> 'Lawyers in the main are intellectual mercenaries to be bought and sold in any cause'

This just fastens on the mercenary nature of professionalism which we discussed earlier. Although the barbs flung at lawyers at this level of criticism normally go for this Achilles' heel, we would suggest that what really excites such critics is the lawyer's dedication to order, regularity, orthodoxy, his unimaginativeness. Whereas the creative artist sees the philistine as someone who draws his gun whenever he hears the word 'culture', his picture of the lawyer is of someone who serves a writ on it.

Sarat also points out a contradiction in society's view of the lawyer. Alongside the artist's distaste for what he perceives, from the viewpoint of his *vie de boheme* or because of his anarchic streak, at the lawyers' staidness, there co-exists suspicion of his trickiness. Swift (also quoted by Sarat) alleged that lawyers were a 'society of men . . . bred from their youth in the art of proving by words, multiplied for purpose, that that which is white is black and black is white, according as they are paid'.

Agents are thought of as self-serving

We have then the general view of the professional as mercenary. There is the literary, derogatory picture of the lawyer as straight-laced and/or devious. But nowadays, the sharpest criticism is at street level. It expresses streetwisdom, the insight or folklore of those who with X-ray eyes can see through all appearances and pretensions. In our context, it emerges from the United States dressed up as 'agency theory', based on research by some US economists. Clive Wolman's report in the *Financial Times* on 14 January 1989 indicates that their 'analysis is built on the rather banal observations that if you get someone else to do a job for you, he will probably rip you off, slacken, pursue his own interests, or fail to seize opportunities unless you watch him very closely'. The thrust of this scepticism is quite clearly that the agent is basically self-serving, or at least weak in his commitment to the principal's interest, despite any theory, protestation, appearance or pretence to the contrary. What it reflects is a modern reluctance to accept things at their face value, in particular to believe in the genuineness of altruism. *A fortiori* – or as the streetwise put it, 'you can say that again' – when the said altruism is combined with commercialism. People believe that the chemistry of such a combination is such that its effect is completely to dissolve away the altruism.

Kidology[4]

The cynicism lying at the bottom of 'agency theory' not only takes in the belief in the centrality of self-interest, but extends beyond that to question the dedication to, or even belief in, the system of the practitioners – in our case, the lawyers – themselves. If there is a current social philosophy, it could well be called kidology. Kidology touches most areas of social intercourse and interaction. Its all-embracing precept is that everything is reducible to self-interest, all else is fake. If we may quote the advice given to a new film actor by Sam Goldwyn, a master of solecisms and high priest of kidology: 'My boy, the most important thing to remember is on honesty. Once you can fake that, you're home'.

In face of this high tide of kidology, a mass turning of backs on, or at least agnosticism as to, ethical values, those qualities such as trust and loyalty and altruism, at the heart of the lawyer-client relationship, were bound to suffer. This did not mean that lawyers had become less trustworthy or more prone

---

4 We should perhaps justify the use of this streetwise term as terminology for the current social phenomenon, which we are about to describe. While we appreciate that its ending is from the Greek, no word wholly derived from a Greek or Latin root would be as fitting.

to breaches of professional ethics, nor that clients ceased to repose trust in their own lawyers. Opinion polls directed at the individual lawyer-client situation show a high level of satisfaction and the complaints statistics, if properly interpreted, tell the same story. Kidology is an ideology, a way of structuring the social world.

Cynicism of lawyers about lawyers

Interestingly, Sarat suggests that cynicism about the legal process affects lawyers themselves. He says:

> 'One of the things that we noted was the frequency with which lawyers criticised or attacked legal institutions and legal officials, the frequency with which lawyers, in their efforts to explain unfavourable outcomes or to control clients' expectations, called into question the competence, motivation and occasionally the integrity of judges and other lawyers.'

It is strange that, if one is convinced of one's own competence, motivation and integrity that one should feel confident in the imputation of the corresponding deficiencies to other lawyers. From another point of view, though, it would be surprising if such a pervasive ideology as modern-day cynicism did not spread to lawyers who, at levels below the judicial, feel bound to make a show at least of streetwisdom. Cynicism is writ large in the media which both reflect and reinforce, that is, feed on and feed the prevailing expectation that cracks lie beneath and will shortly appear in any smooth surface. What is true of new buildings is also true of people in their relationship with others. The exposé journalism of the tabloids fixes on its target and waits impatiently for the crack to show and be photographed. It has been known to use trick photography. The investigative journalism of the quality press is researched and conscientious, but, to some extent even because of such virtues, it too delivers confirmation of the same cynical expectations.

Advertising

Kidology is the dark, the negative, if you like the philosophical, side of current attitudes. The other side is psychological, the sheer gullibility of the same streetwise person as a target of public relations and advertising and promotional material of every kind. His readiness to swallow such material is matched by the advertisers' belief in its efficacy, despite Lord Leverhulme's dictum that half the money spent on advertising was wasted and the only problem was knowing which half was wasted and which was worthwhile[5]. The modern consumer has been described as a self-illusioned hedonist. The garish world of advertising is there to feed his illusions.

Lawyers' advertising

Lawyers, in company with other professionals, have traditionally believed advertising to be unethical. It was close enough to touting to fall under the same ban. ('Touting' is defined in the Solicitor (Scotland) (Advertising) Practice Rules 1987 as 'a direct approach by or on behalf of a solicitor to a person, who is not an established client, with the intention of soliciting business from that person'. The qualification signified by 'direct' in the definition differentiates it from advertising.) Generally, what was struck at was conduct calculated to attract business unfairly. In 1985, two out of three Scottish solicitors had expressed themselves as opposed to advertising in principle. Under government duress, the 1985 Rules allowed advertising, subject to constraints, to avoid the imposition of a regulatory regime by the government. The constraints were substantially relaxed in the 1987 Rules (reproduced in Appendix 4). The generalised prohibition of touting as unfair attraction of business remains in the 1987 Rules. But, the scheme of these Rules is crucially different from that of the Solicitors (Scotland) Practice Rules 1986 (the conflict of interest rules), under which the embargo on representation by a solicitor of two or more parties whose interests conflict is left untouched by the other provisions (cf. p 36). Advertising, provided that it does not stray into the proscribed areas, is deemed not to constitute touting or unfair attraction of

---

5 See article entitled 'A discipline worth "wasting" money on' in the *Financial Times* of 22 June 1989.

business. Presumably, the rationale is that advertising is not a *direct* approach and so is not equivalent to touting. Nor does it attract business *unfairly* since any solicitor is free to advertise. Any solicitor, of course, is also free to chase ambulances.

Personal publicity

In focusing on the attraction of business, what tends to be lost sight of is the discouragement of publicity-seeking by lawyers (see discussion of conflict between self-interest and client's interest, p 18). The Declaration of Perugia 1977 (the predecessor of the CCBE Code) contained what more or less amounted to a total ban on personal publicity. The Code accepts, with evident reluctance, the reality of the permissive publicity regime in the UK, but otherwise retains its frown as regards advertising and personal publicity.

Advertising and image

In this author's view, the impressions conveyed by advertising run directly counter to those select qualities which lawyers seek to cultivate and maintain as constituting their professional reputation. As we saw, though, there is a wide and discouraging gap between the standing in society to which lawyers aspire through the cultivation of that reputation and the lawyers' image. Will the image, then, which has fallen victim to the dark side of kidology revive as a result of the lawyer's embracing of its brighter, other side, self-promotion. So far it has not (witness the media response to the Green Papers despite four years of advertising by lawyers). Nor will it, we believe, in the future. Clients are persons with problems and anxieties, not consumers to be approached through illusions. What requires to be emphasised in the image is the altruism on the lawyer's side in the lawyer-client relationship, not the commercially thrusting features imposed by the government's plastic surgery. That can be achieved only by the ethical pursuit of the client's interest. (See discussion on rekindling of interest in ethics in business concerns and reaction against a view of man as a rational, self-interested calculator in Chapter 6 – the decline of kidology?)

Chapter 6

Independence

The case against codification

It may seem perverse to end a book on professional ethics on a
negative note by opening its last chapter with the case against
codification. Ethics is founded on positive values. In conflicts
between such values, as I have tried to point out, the codes
have usually nothing to say. Worse still, when they do come
down to detailed rules, they are doomed to be misleading.
That is because the details forming the basis for the rule never
quite match the particular facts and circumstances of the ethical problem to be resolved or judged. Indeed, I have already
sought to make that case in criticisms of particular provisions
of some of the codes throughout the rest of the book. The
purpose of this chapter is to show what are the motive forces
behind the pressure for codification, how these are connected
with the social representation or image of the lawyer discussed
in Chapter 5, how codification is related to the independence
of the legal profession and why it is inimical to actual ethical
standards.

Ethics is in fashion

Although it might be too cynical to suggest that ethics is the
flavour of the month, one can certainly say that business has, at
the present time, discovered, or started to rediscover, ethics.
Courses have been set up on ethics for businessmen. A recent
survey found that 42 per cent of the seventy-four UK companies who responded (the questionnaire was sent to the top
200 British companies) said that they had a written code of
ethics of some sort. A few called their document a code of
ethics, but other titles included words like 'principles', 'con-

duct', 'objectives' and 'guidelines'. The objective of these codes was seen by the companies as being to imbue the workforce, from top to bottom, with a code of approved behaviour. The underlying purpose, though, was to create a corporate culture[1]. Our point, of course, is that the behaviour has meaning only in terms of the culture. It is 'approved' or disapproved insofar as it is *culturally* justified. Unless the culture is first absorbed, the regulated behaviour lacks any binding force other than authority.

Criticisms by businessmen

Some businessmen are dismissive of business ethics. 'Business ethics is a contradiction in terms'. A translation of that might be that the businessman's sole objective should be to maximise profits; the values which matter for the businessman are dictated by the market. 'Business is hard enough without bringing ethics into it'. Translation: you have to keep up with, if possible surpass, the competition; you cannot afford to be held back by ethics. (Along similar lines, Sir Sonny Ramphal has put to the richer countries in relation to the North-South divide that the less developed countries, caught up in their struggle to survive, cannot *afford* a luxury like political freedom.) In relation to codes of corporate ethics, a businessman said, 'who can afford time and money to write something that normal people will carry out automatically and bad guys will only ignore?' We would argue that writing it down *helps* the 'bad guys' to 'ignore' it. Furthermore, people are 'normal' in the businessman's sense, provided that they have absorbed the culture to a 'normal' degree.

Culture or system of ethics

This prompts the question whether this book has been about the corporate culture of the legal profession, rather than its system of ethics. The culture, which the companies who

1 This information is contained in *Corporate Codes of Ethics in Large UK Companies*, available free from the Department of Business Studies, University of Edinburgh.

responded to the questionnaire were striving to create, was culture in the sociologist's sense. For our purposes, this could adequately be defined as the shared ideas of a given society. Ethics are concerned with values, not ideas as such. If an ethical statement is challenged, the person who defends it must seek its justification. On the other hand, a challenge to a cultural concept may satisfactorily be met with the assertion that its user is taking it to mean so-and-so and that is the end of the matter. Ideas and values, though, are closely interwoven. Most of our statements are not empirically verifiable, just by looking out of the window so to speak. If we try to justify them, we may well find ourselves doing so by tapping values hidden in the words. For example, as we saw, the fundamentally altruistic nature of the professional responsibility is there within the description 'client'. What is certain is that the ethics of a group or society can be understood only through its culture. (In the article on the movement for reform in the Soviet legal system previously referred to (p 78) Professor Fletcher asks the question whether the Russian lawyers who were now enthusiastic for change had been 'closet liberals' all along. Our suggestion would be that the *cultural* changes had created the concepts and ideas, in terms of which the reform of the legal system could be articulated and justified).

Mission statements

In a study of the mission statements of 75 of America's largest companies (which appeared in the *Long Range Planning Journal*, February 1989), Fred R David gave an illustration of a mission statement. Three labourers were working on a building site. A passer-by asked what they were doing. 'Breaking stones', the first replied. 'Earning a living', the second answered. The third showed a sense of mission. 'Helping to build a cathedral', he said. People outside the US inevitably tend to dismiss the idea of mission statements as some sort of Hollywood hype. Actual mission statements in cold print sound banal. After all, if the building in David's story had been a block of government offices, instead of a building which itself had a 'mission' like a cathedral, his statement would have been taken as no more than a description of the objective. Mission is a large concept, too large perhaps for this side of the Atlantic at this stage in its history (though if people come to believe in a post-1992 United Europe, this may lay a foundation for creation of a sense of mission). The sense of mission is the urge to realise a goal which is envisioned. The vision which inspires the mission will of necessity be broadly defined, vague and, most importantly, far off (but not too far off) in the future. Mission is too overblown a concept, therefore, for the legal practitioner engaged in drafting his pleadings or despatching his formal offer with a 50/50 chance that it will be accepted. What gives him his sense of purpose and direction, instead, are the shared values, culture and philosophy which we have adumbrated in this book.

Big Bang

It is always a relief to come down from Parnassus, especially since the contemporary Parnassus always seems to be located not far from Harvard Business School. We come, though, from the visionary heights of the mission to the even greater concept of Big Bang. Regulation of financial services under the Financial Services Act 1986 accompanied the structural changes in the City of London, which were called the Big Bang. (The metaphor was taken from nothing less than the now favoured theory of the origin of the universe. It was designed to evoke a sense of excitement at the ushering in of a new era. The Stock Market crash of October 1987 was described with an equal modesty as the 'meltdown'. The choice of these terms shows, perhaps, the dominance of the financial centre in today's thinking. This has importance for the independence of the legal profession.) The embrace of the Financial Services Act spread beyond the City into every area of investment business, including insurance. Every lawyer who provides investment advice or conducts investment business must obtain authorisation under, and comply with the provisions of, the Act (see Solicitors (Scotland) (Conduct of Investment Business) Practice Rules 1988). The Act established the watchdog body, the Securities and Investments Board (SIB) and under it a cluster of specialised Self Regulating Organisations (SROs). The SIB produced a rulebook and each SRO had the duty of drawing up its own rulebook which was to provide 'equivalent' investor protection in its own sphere.

Rules or principles

Since its inception, the SIB has been struggling with its rulebook in the face of criticism that it failed to distinguish the different degrees of protection appropriate, respectively, for the professional investor and Aunt Agatha, the investor equivalent of the lawyer's 'man on the Clapham omnibus'. Mainly, and most significantly, though, the rulebooks have been attacked as being 'unnecessarily detailed and and legalistic'. That wording is taken from an article by John Morgan (Chief Executive of the Investment Management Regulatory Organisation (IMRO)) in the *Financial Times* 29 March 1989. He argues for the replacement of rules by principles in a study of the SIB's recently published paper (the paper was related to the DTI's Consultative Document on possible amendments to the Financial Services Act, published at the same time). One of the proposals in the paper is the introduction of Principles of Conduct. Morgan strongly favours the replacement of the present rules by general principles, but claims that the SIB's proposed principles are just their present rules in a different guise. He says: 'There cannot be many pronouncements which meet the criterion of principles. The SIB so far has come up with 104 and are still heading North'. (We would say 'heading South', for it is the law of Scotland which has general principles as its basis while English law is more tied down to particularity.)

What he favours is the segregation of a short list of fundamental principles from the rest of the 104 principles. Such principles, he says, would 'require an observance at all times of high standards of conduct (whereas rules would not, according to one of the main arguments of this book) . . . they [would] represent a collective judgment of what is proper behaviour at all times' (see p 12 for Lord President Emslie's criterion of professional misconduct). He cites with approbation IMRO's General Rule 2.01 that 'members must at all times be fit and proper persons, observing high standards of integrity and fair dealing'.

The SIB's latest proposals in *Regulation of the Conduct of Investment Business*, published on 8 August 1989, adopt Morgan's key idea. What is now proposed is a structure made up of three tiers. The top tier would consist of principles – magically ten – which will inevitably attract the universalist description, the 'ten commandments'; the first commandment, to observe high standards of integrity and fair dealing, signposts its location in the ethical realm. The 46 'core' rules, constituting the middle tier, define the duties of the agent and are applicable to all investment businesses. The function of the third tier is to provide detailed guidance for practitioners under each self-regulating organisation.

Principles plus rules

There is no need for us to chase up further the question whether core or detailed rules are necessary for investor protection in addition to principles. There was strong evidence (e.g. the Guinness and Lloyds scandals) that ethical standards among the investment community had already wilted pre-Big Bang under commercial pressures. The known, indeed the intended, effect of the restructuring in the City was to reinforce these same pressures. The rulebooks would operate to prop up crumbling ethical standards by telling members how to behave in particular circumstances. In the case of legal practice, by contrast, there is a firmly established and well-supported system of ethics (see *post*).

Do rules work?

The City restructuring was designed to facilitate the emergence of integrated financial services houses. In a feature article in *The Business Observer* on 26 February 1989, captioned 'Corporate clients are no longer sure they can trust their financial advisers', Stella Shamoon isolates four areas of concern to corporate clients. (This has certainly no more authority than a media summation of anecdotal evidence. Shamoon acknowledges their subjectivity by leaving open the question whether the areas of concern are 'perceived or real'. But in the nature of things can there be much better evidence, since no-one is likely to be honest about their dishonesty to researchers and no-one knows what percentage, if any, are found out). The areas are:

'Potential conflicts of interest within integrated full-service houses, with the self-interest of often publicly-quoted, bottom-line oriented advisers, possibly taking precedence over the client's best interests (cf. p 17 for the paramountcy of client's interest over self-interest in legal ethics);

Price-sensitive information may leak through chinese walls from corporate financiers to market-makers (see Chapter 3 on Confidentiality);

Broker analysts are under pressure to come up with 'stories' for the sales, market-making and corporate finance teams within their integrated organisations. The 'independence of much broker research is thus suspect in the eyes of professional investors, . . . (see this chapter *post* on independence of the legal profession);

The structure of the banking industry post-Big Bang, with a handful of major houses commanding a lion's share of corporate business, exacerbates potential conflicts of loyalty' (the Green Paper proposals, if implemented, may by themselves, even if the separate idea of multi-disciplinary practices is dropped, create legal mega-practices with the same consequences).

Are rules and principles of conduct for the benefit of clients?

Under s 62 of the Financial Services Act 1986, breaches of the rules have implications both for discipline and civil liability. To come nearer home, however, we should study the basic philosophy of an article entitled 'Ten Commandments' by Ruth Adler ((1988) 33 JLSS 250). The writer asks the question: 'What ought lay people to expect from solicitors?' This, from the lay side, coincides, but only partially, with the question from the lawyer's angle: 'What is a good solicitor?' From two answers to her question, she purports to derive 'Ten commandments and principles'. The answers, particularly, blur the already smudged boundary line between competence and ethics (cf. p 61). That is inevitable since the good solicitor would exhibit both skill and high ethical standards. Looked at from the client's point of view, also, the client would want to see both of these attributes. Indeed, Ruth Adler, in her capacity as assistant to the Lay Observer, will naturally have formulated her answers by generalising from the solicitors' alleged inadequacies in complaints to the Lay Observer. As generalisations, they escape the pitfalls of the detailed codes, but what is one to make of a proposition that a client is entitled to expect 'that information and advice tendered will be *correct*' (Ruth Adler's italics). In calling for 'correct' advice Ruth Adler goes even beyond the requirement of the FIMBRA (Financial Intermediaries, Managers and Brokers Regulatory Association) for 'best advice' (a cynic has suggested that what the FIMBRA rules amount to is best advice, on how an intermediary recommending, say, a Barlow Clowes Fund could best avoid being sued). The ten commandments and principles are supposed to be drawn from the answers to the opening questions. From the tenth commandment, 'Thou shalt honour thy profession . . .', is generated the principle: 'Always act in such a way as to uphold the independence, integrity and reputation of the profession as a whole'. This is a good statement in naive form of an aspirational principle, which will be followed by the good lawyer. (This criticism is not as sharp as it sounds. No 'commandment' or aspirational principle can be expressed other than naively.) It seems unreal, though, to derive it from expectations on the client's side.

Need for a code?

In her preamble, Ruth Adler, echoing the Lay Observer (although the Lay Observer in her Tenth Annual Report (para 6 of Introduction) had indicated that most complaints fell into 'the grey area of incomptence and poor work') takes as obvious the proposition that her exercise 'in no way vitiates the need for a written code of conduct, whether on the English model or on some more specifically Scottish pattern, such as that offered by *The Websters*'. But *The Websters*, on the contrary, explicitly endorse (p 2) the Law Society's attitude that 'a few general rules (this presumably means 'principles') should be observed in the spirit'. *The Websters* in no way constitutes a code in any sense (see below for definition) and certainly not in the form and substance called for by the Lay Observer and pressed for by the government. (The status of *The Websters*'

Seven Pillars of Wisdom (p 50) is that of '*general* ethical rules' – their description, author's italics. The difference in the concepts unconsciously embodied in their chosen metaphors is interesting. 'Pillars of wisdom' suggests not the idea of a handing down from above by an omnipotent consumer inherent in the concept of a 'commandment', but the Aristotelian notion of the right-thinking man working out the principles of a good life).

International and Community codes

The International Code of Ethics adopted by the International Bar Association in 1956 (and later amended) is barely a code. We take a code to be a statement of law or other normative rules arranged with the broadest generalisation at the head and proceeding from there in descending order of generality. The International Code is presented in the familiar format of a set of principles (20 this time), to each of which is appended brief illustrative material or a restatement of a preceding positive principle in negative form (an example: 'Lawyers shall at all times maintain the honour and dignity of their profession. They shall, in practice as well as in private life, abstain from any behaviour which may tend to discredit the profession of which they are members'). The Declaration of Perugia 1977, the predecessor of the CCBE Code, did not describe its subject-matter as a 'Code of Ethics' but as 'Principles of Professional Conduct'. These were designed to be European Community-wide (the EC as it was then constituted). The CCBE Code of Conduct is designed for lawyers in the EC (as now constituted) and substantially restates and develops the principles of the Declaration of Perugia. The CCBE Code does not fit the definition of a code, as does not the International Code. They are, just like the 'Ten Commandments' and 'Seven Pillars of Wisdom', arrangements of ethical principles. Moreover, terms such as 'rules' and 'principles', and 'ethics' and 'conduct', which ought to be strictly differentiated, are instead permutated indiscriminately. Paradoxically, the principle which we have just taken as an example from the International Code of *Ethics* in substance regulates *conduct*. Its equivalent in the CCBE Code of Conduct is *ethical* in substance.

Independence

At the beginning of this chapter, we undertook to show the relationship between codification of ethics or rules of conduct and the independence of the legal profession. The proposition that independence is of the essence reverberates throughout all of the collections of principles which we have mentioned. We must now explore what an independent legal profession involves.

Problem of lawyer-client communication

If anything demonstrates the problem of communication between lawyers and their clients it is the baffling, sometimes exasperating, mismatch between the lawyer's good, or not so good, work and the client's appreciation or criticism of it. Not infrequently, eyebrows are raised and consciences twitch in lawyers' offices when a letter of fulsome appreciation comes from a client, whose excessive phone calls have been dreaded and to whom, as a result, services have been grudgingly rendered. This is at least balanced, if not outweighed, by the silences, or sometimes even complaints, from other clients, in whose interest a difficult point has been won or an unmeritedly good result achieved. Not only do clients' responses or lack of response often not fit events in the real legal world, but it is nearly always difficult to know how such responses or unresponsiveness are to be interpreted. A client may trust his lawyer in the way and to the extent necessary for a good going lawyer-client relationship but his attitude of trust need not include sincerity. Silence where appreciation would be fitting may mean that the client does not want to risk an appreciation (the pun *is* intended) in the fee. It can be, instead, that the fulsome expression of gratitude is deviously intended as a substitute for the fee. There is corresponding reserve on the lawyer's side. Some clients are regarded as good to work for, some are not.

Client's dependence on lawyer

We have said before that, although the lawyer pursues the client's interest which must be paramount over the lawyer's self-interest, that does not amount to identification. The lawyer carries the professional responsibility. The client is, therefore, inevitably dependent on the lawyer. The relationship, stops short of identification and is not at all reciprocal. It follows from the client's dependence within the relationship that the lawyer's stance in relation to the client requires to be altruistic. It is imperative that the lawyer guards against dependence on the client. It is in that negative sense only that Ruth Adler is logically entitled to 'deduce' the lawyer's independence from her question, 'What ought the client to expect from the lawyer' (see p 135). The wrong type of lawyer-client relationship is perhaps best expressed idiomatically in the form that the client should not have the lawyer 'in his pocket'. The legendary Chicago gangster – at least according to the Hollywood version – invariably included his attorney in his entourage. He acted as his 'mouthpiece', he 'sprang' him from jail. His ethics rose no higher than those of his master. Unlike Dershowitz, he did not abjure unfair means or even illegality.

Types of dependence

Dependence can develop in many ways. Some persons are subservient, some dominate, by nature. For some lawyers, therefore, an undesirable degree of dependence, where it rests on such a psychological predisposition, may be unavoidable. It is unnecessary to distinguish the psychologically dependent lawyer from the lawyer who too closely identifies himself with the client (it is the client's *interest* with which the lawyer should identify himself). The lawyer who fantasises his role into that of a white knight on a black charger riding to the rescue of a fair maiden – his client – lacks the right degree of professional detachment, just as if he were psychologically dependent on the client. Psychology apart, we can isolate four other sources of dependence.

Close ties

A person, a lawyer included, who acts for himself has a fool for a client. Underlying the truism is the point that the value attached to independent advice has been renounced. The same deprivation of truly independent advice may result, sometimes to a greater extent, where the lawyer acts for relatives or close friends. The hazard is greater in the case of a legal problem, where advice or counsel is sought, than with transactions.

Et dona ferentes

Virgil warned that the Greeks are to be feared even when they are bringing gifts. This might be paraphrased to the effect that clients should be regarded with caution *especially* when they bear gifts. Lavish presents or lavish praise, even more so a heady combination of the two, may seduce the lawyer into excessive subservience to the client. Token gifts and a due measure of gratitude should not. Different lawyers have different susceptibilities.

Power

Many people, and therefore many lawyers, are impressed by power. From power, its possessors derive a belief in their own judgments, right or wrong, an expectation of automatic obedience by others and a dislike of independence of thought or values on the part of those who serve them. If the possessor of power seeks out a lawyer who is impressed by power, the proper distribution of dependence within the lawyer-client relationship will be upset. This is exemplified by the Chicago gangster-mouthpiece relationship.

Money

By money here, we mean enough to create at the client's end of the relationship an aura of freespending and glamour. Power nowadays is often associated with or derived from money. But money alone can cast its spell. The possessor of money in the sense here described is likely to be a person who has developed the attitude that everything within sight or within the scope of desire can be bought. Such an attitude can extend to legal services and then directly to the provider of them. The lawyer becomes a commodity. This does not mean that, on the lawyer's side, he is lured by the prospect of easy money, that is, large fees easily earned. (There may, indeed, be an inverse relationship between the possession of money and the readiness to distribute largesse.) The psychological factor at work to erode the lawyer's independence is the *importance* attached to money, which is reflected on to its possessor.

Two-way independence

A government junior minister was reported recently as having made the comment that some of the IRA men's lawyers were 'unduly sympathetic' to their clients. The statement is capable of two interpretations. One points in the direction of the Chicago gangster syndrome. The minister may have been suggesting that the lawyers' independence had been subverted, like the attorneys in the gangsters' entourage, but in the IRA men's lawyers' case through a clandestine or latent attachment to the IRA cause. But the remark could be differently construed as meaning that the lawyers were not sufficiently influenced by the concern of the authorities. In view of the overpowering public interest in success in the battle against terrorism[2], the lawyers should have pursued their clients' defence according to a modified set of rules, the thrust of which would have been more truth-seeking (equivalent to the more even-handed approach of the prosecuting lawyer in a criminal trial). On that construction, the suggestion would be completely improper (as it would be on

2 By its recent ban on media interviews with Sinn Fein members the government has demonstrated its belief in the strength of the public interest in this sphere. It is a classic case of conflict of ethical values, in this case between freedom of speech and the suppression of crime. Once the nature of the contest is seen to shift from the prevention and detection of crime to 'war' or 'battle', there is pressure to change the rules; cf. Chapter 4 at p 80.

the other interpretation if there was no *evidence* of illegality or adoption of unfair means). Even more important than the duty to remain independent of the client is the legal profession's independence of the authorities.

Green Papers

The Green Papers[3] (three for England and Wales and one for Scotland) containing proposals for consultation with the legal profession were published by the government in early 1989. The cynicism of lawyers about lawyers (cf. p 125; particularly lawyers turned politician perhaps, such as the Prime Minister, the Lord Chancellor and the Secretary of State for Scotland) perhaps underlay the titling of the Papers as proposals for the 'reform' of the legal profession. 'Reform' suggests some sort of present delinquency or deep deficiency. For our purposes[3] the most significant comment of all was the Lord Chancellor's statement in introducing the proposals that the legal system was too important to be left to the lawyers.

Attack on lawyers' independence

The Lord Chancellor's assertion heralded a three-pronged attack in the Green Papers on lawyers' independence. One, commercialism was to be reinforced. Two, the government was to take powers which would enable it to control both the levels of competence and standards of conduct. Three, the professional relationship was to be forced in the direction of a lawyer-consumer relationship, instead of a lawyer-client relationship.

3 I do not propose to criticise the Green Paper proposals in any detail. At the time of writing they have appeared in a modified form in a White Paper (Legal Services: A Framework for the Future, July 1989, Cm 740) for England and Wales and 'The Scottish Legal Profession: the Way Forward' by the Scottish Home and Health Department.

Commercialism

The proposals would mean that solicitors would require to market their services competitively with other providers of similar services. Solicitor-advocates would vie commercially with independent advocates. Solicitors would pit themselves against one another, with the emphasis put on marketing ability, presentational skills and access to publicity. It is axiomatic in the writer's view that concentration on the commercial dimension in these ways leads inevitably to a decline in professionalism. Scattered throughout this book are instances of such an inverse relationship between commercialism and professionalism. Basically, the process of marketing involves a shift of focus to the promotion of the lawyer's self-interest from the pursuit of the client's interest. By the subjection of the lawyer to stronger market forces, his professional independence would be threatened.

Government control

The Green Papers implicitly recognised that the intensification of competition has the potential to undermine professional responsibility in both areas, skills and ethics. The logically obvious conclusion is not drawn that it would be better not to stoke up the competitive forces which already operate. Instead, what was proposed was the creation of powers for the government to redraw the lines of professional responsibility. It would be able to make regulations which would determine the standards of entry, training, practice and conduct. It would have power both to settle and control the supervision of standards. The actual supervision of standards of conduct would be left with the Discipline Tribunal. But the setting of the standards, including prescriptions for conduct, would be under the control of the government[4].

---

4 This drew a warning from Robert D Raven, President of the American Bar Association, who was reported to have said: 'We would . . . be extremely concerned about the proposal that our code of professional conduct, which is a testament to the principles of self-regulation and independence, could be subject to the approval of Congress'.

Advisory function

The control which was to have been exercised by the government under the Green Paper proposals has, in the White Paper, been scaled down to an advisory function. That function, moreover, is to be fulfilled by an independent quango, chaired by a senior judge. A bare majority of this committee will be lay persons. The initial debate has centred on whether or not these structural changes amount to a backing down by the government. Rather than that shallow question, the important points are the nature and extent of the influence which the committee will seek, or has the authority to exert, on the ethos of the profession and how the committee's own philosophy will be forged from the interaction between the legal and the lay members. These questions are unanswerable. What can be said with certainty, though, is that the institution of a lay-controlled committee above the professional bodies must remain for the future a lurking threat to professional independence.

Fostering of lawyer-consumer relationships

It is proposed that the Lay Observer (as he now is), in the guise of the Legal Ombudsman (as he then would be) be given powers, in parallel with the court's existing jurisdiction which would presumably continue, to order compensation for clients who claimed to have suffered loss at the hands of lawyers. In the case of inadequate work, the Ombudsman would wield the Law Society's present powers under the Solicitors (Scotland) Act 1988 (see p 28). It is not made clear whether these powers of the Ombudsman would be alternative to, or in substitution for, those conferred by that statute on the Law Society.

Implementation of these proposals would provide a unique (so far as we are aware) occasion for the system of justice to be sidetracked in matters of compensation for alleged breaches of contract. (The contrast with the continental system and practice is startling. In France it is possible to sue a lawyer for negligence, but it has apparently never happened, and in Brussels the general view is that it is impossible. The client's remedy is not to use the same lawyer again.) The potential for harassment by malcontents and paranoid clients is horrifying. That is particularly so, since the intensified competition to attract clients aimed at by the other proposals is bound to lead to solicitor-client relations with shallower roots. Indeed, the enactment of the proposals, because they will bring yet another security agency, so to speak, on to the scene, will itself tend to undermine the exchange of trust on which the lawyer-client relationship is founded. Beyond a certain point, the more policemen there are about and the fiercer are the watchdogs, the less secure will people feel.

Under the proposals, lay persons would become judges of lawyers' competence. The definition of 'inadequate professional services' uses as a criterion the quality of services reasonably to be expected of a 'competent' solicitor (s 5(1) of the 1988 Act). Inadequate work is taken to be an outward manifestation of incompetence. But the proposition now taken for granted by the court is that the guardians of the standards of competence and reputable conduct are 'competent and reputable solicitors', who alone can judge whether there has been a departure from these standards (cf. p 12 and *MacColl v Council of the Law Society of Scotland* 1987 SLT 525). Any attempt to define competence by any other criterion is foredoomed (see discussion of weaknesses of Law Society's 'working definition' of competence p 59).

Dangerous philosophy of proposals

What is most disturbing is the philosophy which underlies the proposals. The qualities of altruism, integrity and independence, on which the *standing* of the lawyer in society relies, require continuous reassertion and reinforcement. The three-pronged thrust of the Green Papers, which we have identified earlier in this chapter, would work against that process. Not only that, but the greatest irony would be that the poor image of the lawyer, which has been exploited to support and justify the proposals, would in turn be fortified by their operation. From a broader perspective, we can see that the proposals pick up on social trends which have been developing for some two decades at least. These are kidology, consumerism, commercialism, populism (see *The Lawyer and Society* Chapter 6 *passim* for discussion of the influence of these trends on the working of the legal system). But, here and there, counterstatements are now appearing which indicate a different way ahead.

Legal counterstatement

The CCBE Code adds up to a counterstatement in the field of professional ethics. It picks out common values. Although its principles represent the lowest common denominator of the principles of the systems of legal professional ethics in the member countries, its philosophy is intended to shape revisions of national rules 'with the view to their progressive harmonisation' (virtually all of the Green Paper proposals diverge from the Code's principles on almost every major issue).

Social counterstatements

We have already pointed out (p 128) the surge of resurgence of interest in ethics in business. Some, at least, of these ethical codes embody duties related to the environment, so reflecting community if not global concerns. Here we have a shift not only from the narrow perspective of self-interest but also away from the tyranny of short-term calculation. Perhaps, even more significantly, fundamental thinkers are beginning to question the theoretical foundations, to which kidology is the street parallel. In *Passion Within Reason* (Norton, 1989), Robert Frank robustly states the case:

> 'In recent years, the message from behavioural scientists has been that people are fundamentally selfish. Biologists tell us that behaviour is shaped ultimately by material rewards . . . Psychologists affirm this view . . . Economists, for their part, point with pride to the power of self-interest to explain and predict behaviour, not only in the world of commerce but in networks of personal relationships as well.'[5]

5 Richard Posner, a Chicago Professor of Law and a Federal Judge, has developed an economic analysis of law.

Yet, he states,

'The plain fact is that many people do not fit the me-first caricature.'

Centrality of professional ethics

Frank reports on an experiment run by psychologists at Yale to see how far students behaved like rational egoists. One finding of great interest was that students of commerce and economics were much more likely than students of other subjects to conform to the selfish paradigm. This is a strong pointer to the conclusion that persons brought up on a diet of ideas based on the assumption that man always acts in accordance with self-interest will come to believe that it is only reasonable to be selfish. The study of professional ethics, at the heart of which is altruism – the very antithesis of self-interest – is the strongest possible counter-statement to such perversity.

Appendices

Appendix 1

Solicitors (Scotland) Accounts Rules 1989

Rules made by the Council of the Law Society of Scotland under sections 34, 35 and 36 of the Solicitors (Scotland) Act 1980 on 28th April 1989.

Citation
1. (1) These Rules may be cited as the Solicitors (Scotland) Accounts Rules 1989.

Commencement and repeal
(2) In these Rules shall come into operation on the first day of June 1989 and from that date the Solicitors (Scotland) Accounts Rules 1986, shall cease to have effect.

Interpretation
2. (1) In these Rules, unless the context otherwise requires:—
'the Act' means the Solicitors (Scotland) Act 1980;
'bank' means the Bank of England, a Trustee Savings Bank within the meaning of section 54 of the Trustee Savings Bank Act 1981, the National Savings Bank, the Post Office in the exercise of its powers to provide banking services and an authorised institution within the meaning of the Banking Act 1987 and which operates within the bankers automated clearing system provided however that a recognised bank not operating within the bankers automated clearing system may be approved by the Council for the purposes of this sub-section;
'client account' means a current, deposit, savings account or other form of account or a deposit receipt at a branch of a bank in the United Kingdom in the name of the solicitors in the title of which the word 'client', 'trustee', 'trust' or other fiduciary term appears and includes an account or a deposit receipt with a bank, a deposit, share or other account with a Building Society designated under Section 1 of the House Purchase and Housing Act 1959, a current or general account with a building society operating such an account within the

149

bankers automated clearing system or an account showing sums on loan to a local authority being in such cases in name of the solicitor for a client whose name is specified in the title of the account or receipt;

'clients' money' means money (not belonging to him) received by a solicitor whether as a solicitor or as a trustee in the course of his practice;

'the Council' means the Council of the Society;

'Faculty' means a faculty or society of solicitors in Scotland incorporated by Royal Charter or otherwise formed in accordance with law, but does not include the Society;

'local authority' means a local authority within the meaning of the Local Government (Scotland) Act 1973;

'partner' means a member of a firm of solicitors or a director or member of an incorporated practice;

'print out' means a printed or typewritten copy of any account or other information stored in a computer;

'the Society' means the Law Society of Scotland, established under the Act;

'solicitor' means a solicitor holding a practising certificate under the Act and includes a firm of solicitors and an incorporated practice under section 34(1)(a) of the Act;

(2) The Interpretation Act 1978 applies to the interpretation of these Rules as it applies to the interpretation of an Act of Parliament.

Rules not to apply to solicitors in certain employments
3. These Rules shall not apply to a solicitor who is in any of the employments mentioned in sub-section (4)(a), (b) and (c) of section 35(1) of the Act so far as regards moneys received, held or paid by him in the course of that employment.

Clients' money to be paid into client account
4. (1) Subject to the provisions of Rule 7 every solicitor shall:—

(a) ensure that at all times the sum at the credit of the client account, or where there are more such accounts than one, the total of the sums at the credit of those accounts shall not be less than the total of the clients' money held by the solicitor and

(b) pay into a client account without delay any sum of money exceeding £50 held for or received from or on behalf of a client.

(2) Where money is held by the solicitor in a client account in which the name of the client is specified and where no money is due to that client by the solicitor or the amount due is less than the amount in the specified client account the sum in that account or, as the case may be, the excess, shall not be treated as clients' money for the purposes of paragraph (1)(a) of this Rule.

(3) Nothing herein contained shall:—

(a) empower a solicitor, without the express written authority of the client, to deposit any money held by the solicitor for that client with a bank or on share, deposit or other account with a building society or on loan account with a local authority in name of the solicitors for that client except on such terms as will enable the amount of the share or deposit or loan or any part thereof to be uplifted or withdrawn on notice not exceeding one calendar month;

(b) relieve a solicitor of his responsibility to the client to ensure that all sums belonging to that client and held in a client account in terms of these Rules are available when required for that client or for that client's purpose; and

(c) preclude the overdrawing by a solicitor of a client account in which the name of the client for whom it is held is specified where that client has given written authority to overdraw; an overdraft on such account shall not be taken into account to ensure compliance with paragraph (1)(a) of this Rule.

Other payments to client account

5. There may be paid into a client account:—

(a) such money belonging to the solicitor as may be necessary for the purpose of opening the account or required to ensure compliance with Rule 4(1)(a);

(b) money to replace any sum which may by mistake or accident have been withdrawn from the account.

Drawings from client account

6. (1) So long as money belonging to one client is not withdrawn without his written authority for the purpose of meeting a payment to or on behalf of another client, there may be drawn from a client account—

(a) money required for payment to or on behalf of a client;

(b) money required for or to account of payment of a debt due to the solicitor by a client or in or to account of repayment of money expended by the solicitor on behalf of a client;

(c) money drawn on a client's authority;

(d) money properly required for or to account of payment of the solicitor's professional account against a client which has been debited to the ledger account of the client in the solicitor's books;

(e) money for transfer to a separate client account kept or to be kept for the client only;

(f) money which may have been paid into the account under paragraph (a) of Rule 5 and which is no longer required to ensure compliance with Rule 4(1)(a); and

(g) money which may by mistake or accident have been paid into the account.

Exceptions from Rule 4

7. Notwithstanding any of the provisions of these Rules, a solicitor shall not be obliged to pay into a client account but shall be required to record in his books clients' money held or received by him:—

(a) in the form of cash which is without delay paid in cash in the ordinary course of business to the client or a third party on the client's behalf; or

(b) in the form of a cheque or draft which is endorsed over in the ordinary course of business to the client or to a third party on the client's behalf and which is not passed by the solicitor through a bank account; or

(c) which he pays without delay into a separate bank, building society or local authority deposit account opened or to be opened in name of the client or of some person named by the client; or

(d) which the client for his own convenience has requested the solicitor in writing to withhold from such account; or

(e) for or to account of payment of a debt due to the solicitor from the client or in repayment in whole or in part of money expended by the solicitor on behalf of the client; or

(f) expressly on account of a professional account incurred by the client, or as an agreed fee or to account of an agreed fee for business done for the client.

Bridging loans

8. A solicitor shall not enter into or maintain any contract or arrangement with a bank or other lender in terms of which the solicitor may draw down loan or overdraft facilities in his name for behoof of clients unless:—

(1) the solicitor shall in every case before drawing down any sums in terms of such contract or arrangement have intimated in writing to the bank or other lender—

(a) the name and present address of the client for whom the loan or overdraft facilities are required; and

(b) the arrangements for repayment of the loan or overdraft facilities; and

(2) the contract or arrangement does not impose personal liability for repayment of any such loan or overdraft facilities on the solicitor.

Borrowing from clients
9. A solicitor shall not borrow money from his client unless his client is in the business of lending money or his client has been independently advised in regard to the making of the loan.

Accounts required to be kept in books of solicitor
10. (1) A solicitor shall at all times keep properly written up such books and accounts as are necessary:—
  (a) to show all his dealing with:—
    (i) clients' money held or received or paid or in any way intromitted with by him; and
    (ii) any other money dealt with by him through a client account; and
    (iii) any bank overdrafts or loans procured by him in his own name for behoof of a client or clients;
    (iv) any other money held by the solicitor in a separate account in the title of which the client's name is specified.
  (b) (i) to show separately in respect of each client all money of the categories specified in sub-paragraph (a) of this paragraph which is received, held or paid by him on account of that client; and
    (ii) to distinguish all money of the said categories received, held or paid by him from any other money received, held or paid by him.
(2) All dealings referred to in sub-paragraph (1) of this Rule shall be recorded as may be appropriate:—
  (a) either in a clients' cash book, or a clients' column of a cash book, and
  (b) in a clients' ledger or a clients' column of a ledger.
(3) A solicitor shall at all times keep properly written up such books and accounts as are necessary to show the true financial position of his practice.
(4) The 'books', 'accounts', 'ledger' and 'records' referred to in these Rules shall be deemed to include loose-leaf books and such cards or other permanent records as are necessary for the operation of any system of book-keeping, mechanical or computerised, and
(5) Where a solicitor maintains the accounts required by these Rules on a computerised system which does not rely on a visible ledger card for its operation such system must be such that:—
  (a) an immediate printout can be obtained of any account notwithstanding that immediate visual access is available; and
  (b) all accounts which for any reason may require to be removed from the working store of the system must before removal be copied on to a storage medium which will enable a visual record of the

detailed entries therein to be produced and be filed in alphabetical or other suitable order, indexed and retained for the period set out in Rule 10(6) hereof.

(6) A solicitor shall preserve for at least ten years from the date of the last entry therein all books and accounts kept by him under this Rule or a copy thereof in a form which will enable a visible record of the detailed entries therein to be produced from such a copy.

Client bank statements to be regularly reconciled

11. (1) Every solicitor shall within one month of the coming into force of these Rules or of his commencing practice on his own account (either alone or in partnership or an incorporated practice) whichever shall be the later, and thereafter at intervals not exceeding one month cause the balance between the client bank lodged and drawn columns of his cash book or the balance on his client bank ledger account as the case may be to be agreed with his client bank statements and shall retain such reconciliation statements showing this agreement for a period of eighteen months from the dates they were respectively carried out; and

(2) at the same date or dates extract from his clients' ledger a list of balances due by him to clients and prepare a statement comparing the total of the said balances with the reconciled balance in the client bank account and retain such lists of balances and statements for a period of eighteen months from the dates they were respectively carried out.

Client funds invested in specified accounts

12. (1) Every solicitor shall at the end of his accounting period following the coming into force of these Rules or of his commencing practice on his own account (either alone or in partnership or an incorporated practice) whichever shall be the later and thereafter at intervals not exceeding twelve months cause the balance between the client deposited and withdrawn columns of his cash book or the balance on his client invested funds ledger account as the case may be to be agreed with his client passbooks, building society printouts, special deposit accounts, local authority deposits or other statements or certificates and shall retain such reconciliation statements showing this agreement for a period of eighteen months from the dates they were respectively carried out: and

(2) at the same date extract from his client ledger a list of funds invested by him in his name for specified clients and prepare a statement comparing the total of the said balances with the reconciled investment funds and retain such lists of balances and statements for a period of eighteen months from the dates they were respectively carried out.

Interest to be earned for a client

13. (1) Where a solicitor holds money for or on account of a client and, having regard to the amount of such money and the length of time for which it or any part of it is likely to be held, it is reasonable that interest should be earned for the client, the solicitor shall so soon as practicable place money or, as the case may be, such part thereof in a separate interest bearing client account in the title of which the client's name is specified and shall account to the client for any interest earned thereon, failing which the solicitor shall pay to the client out of his own money a sum equivalent to the interest which would have accrued for the benefit of the client if the sum he ought to have placed in such an interest bearing client account under this Rule had been so placed.

(2) Without prejudice for the generality of paragraph (1) of this Rule it shall be deemed reasonable that interest should be earned for a client from the date on which a solicitor receives for or on account of the client a sum of money not less than £500 which at the time of its receipt is unlikely within two months thereafter to be either wholly disbursed or reduced by payments to a sum less than £500.

(3) Without prejudice to any other remedy which may be available to him, any client who feels aggrieved that interest has not been paid to him under this Rule shall be entitled to require the solicitor to obtain a certificate from the Society as to whether or not interest ought to have been earned for him and, if so, the amount of such interest and upon the issue of such certificate any interest certified to be due shall be payable by the solicitor to the client.

(4) Nothing in this Rule shall affect any arrangement in writing, whenever made, between a solicitor and his client as to the application of a client's money or interest thereon.

Investigation of accounts on behalf of Council

14. (1) To enable them to ascertain whether or not these Rules are being complied with, the Council may by written notice require any solicitor to produce at a time to be fixed by the Council and at a place to be fixed by the Council, or in the option of the solicitor at his place of business, his books of account, bank passbooks, loose-leaf bank statements, deposit receipts, building society passbooks, local authority deposits, separate statements of bank overdrafts or loans procured by him in his own name for behoof of a client or clients, statements of account, vouchers and any other necessary documents including magnetic storage disks and microfilm records (in this Rule referred to as 'books and other documents') for the inspection of a person appointed by the Council being a professional accountant.

(2) A solicitor duly required to do so under paragraph (1) of this

Rule shall produce such books and other documents at the time and place fixed.

(3) The person appointed by the Council to make the inspection shall investigate the solicitor's books and other documents with the object of ascertaining whether or not these Rules are being complied with by the solicitor, and thereafter shall report to the Council upon the result of his inspection.

(4) In any case in which a Faculty request that an inspection should be made under this Rule of the books and other documents of a solicitor, such Faculty shall transmit to the Council a statement containing all relevant information in their possession and a request that such an inspection be made.

(5) A written notice given by the Council to a solicitor under paragraph (1) and where appropriate paragraph (6) of this Rule shall be signed by the Secretary, a Deputy Secretary or the Chief Accountant of the Society and sent by recorded delivery service to the solicitor at his place of business as defined in the constitution of the Society or in the case of a solicitor who has ceased to hold a practising certificate at his last known address, and shall be deemed to have been received by the solicitor within forty-eight hours of the time of posting. In the case of a firm or incorporated practice the written notice shall be given to each person who is known to the Council to be a partner of the firm or director of the incorporated practice and it shall not be necessary to give notice to the firm or incorporated practice also.

(6) Where following an inspection of the books and other documents of a solicitor in terms of paragraph (1) of this Rule it appears to the Council that the solicitor has not complied with these Rules and the Council instructs a further inspection of the books and other documents of the solicitor, the Council may by written notice require the solicitor to pay to the Council such sum as may be required to meet the fees and costs incurred by the Council in carrying out such further inspection, provided always that such written notice is given to the solicitor not more than one year after the date of the inspection first referred to in this paragraph. The amount of such sum shall be fixed by the Council and intimated to the solicitor following such inspection.

(7) It shall be the duty of a solicitor upon whom a notice in terms of paragraph (6) of this Rule has been served to make payment forthwith of the amounts so intimated.

(8) Any sum paid to the Council in terms of paragraph (7) hereof shall accrue to the Guarantee Fund.

Application of Rules in case of firm of solicitors
15. Each partner of a firm of solicitors shall be responsible for securing compliance by the firm with the provisions of these Rules.

Savings of right of solicitor against client
16. Nothing in these Rules shall deprive a solicitor of or prejudice
him with reference to any recourse or right in law, whether by way
of lien, set-off, counter-claim, charge or otherwise, against moneys
standing to the credit of a client account or against moneys due to a
client by a third party.

Solicitors (Scotland) Act 1988

1. After section 42 of the Solicitors (Scotland) Act 1980 (in this Act referred to as 'the 1980 Act') there shall be inserted the following sections—

42A. Powers where inadequate professional services alleged

(1) Where—
    (a) the Council receive, from any person having an interest, a complaint that professional services provided by a solicitor in connection with any matter in which he has been instructed by a client were inadequate; and
    (b) the Council, after inquiry and after giving the solicitor an opportunity to make representations, uphold the complaint,
they may take such of the steps mentioned in subsection (2) as they think fit.

(2) The steps referred to in subsection (1) are—
    (a) to determine that the amount of the fees and outlays to which the solicitor shall be entitled for the services shall be—
        (i) nil; or
        (ii) such amount as the Council may specify in the determination,
and to direct the solicitor to comply, or secure compliance, with such of the requirements set out in subsection (3) as appear to them to be necessary to give effect to the determination;
    (b) to direct the solicitor to secure the rectification at his own expense of any such error, omission or other deficiency arising in connection with the services as the Council may specify;
    (c) to direct the solicitor to take, at his own expense, such other action in the interests of the client as the Council may specify.

(3) The requirements referred to in subsection (2)(a) are—

(a) to refund, whether wholly or to any specified extent, any amount already paid by or on behalf of the client in respect of the fees and outlays of the solicitor in connection with the services;

(b) to waive, whether wholly or to any specified extent, the right to recover those fees and outlays.

.   .   .

5.—(1) In section 65(1) of the 1980 Act (interpretation), after the definition of 'functions' there shall be inserted the following definition—

' "inadequate professional services" means professional services which are in any respect not of the quality which could reasonably be expected of a competent solicitor, and cognate expressions shall be construed accordingly; and references to the provision of inadequate professional services shall be construed as including references to not providing professional services which such a solicitor ought to have provided;'.

Appendix 3

Law Society of Scotland Competence Committee Report to Council

After a very full discussion, the Committee arrived at the following working definition of the competent solicitor, based closely on that put forward in 1982 by the American Law Institute–American Bar Association:—

'The competent solicitor:—
(i) deals with business with appropriate speed;
(ii) is specifically knowledgeable about the fields of law in which he or she practises, and maintains that knowledge through regular attendance at relevant continuing legal education courses or by other means;
(iii) exercises an appropriate level of skill in these fields of law;
(iv) exercises reasonable care;
(v) maintains effective office systems;
(vi) communicates effectively with clients;
(vii) identifies and avoids the areas of practice in which he or she does not have the knowledge or skill to deal effectively.'

It should be understood, however, that the Committee's notion of competence is relative, and it accepts that, for example, it would be quite inappropriate to impose the standards relevant to the specialist on the general practitioner. A departure by a solicitor from the Committee definition of competence need not by itself indicate incompetence, which will be a matter of degree and frequency in each case. Competence, in other words, should not be seen to be synonymous with excellence, since this would cause difficulties in identifying appropriate solutions to problems of incompetence.

Solicitors (Scotland) (Advertising) Practice Rules 1987

Rules dated 28th May 1987, made by the Council of the Law Society of Scotland and approved by the Lord President of the Court of Session in terms of section 34 of the Solicitors (Scotland) Act 1980.

1.—(1) These rules may be cited as the Solicitors (Scotland) (Advertising) Practice Rules 1987.

(2) These rules shall come into operation on 1st July 1987.

2.—(1) In these rules, unless the context otherwise requires—

'the Act' means the Solicitors (Scotland) Act 1980;

'the Council' means the Council of the Society;

'established client' means a person for whom a solicitor has acted on at least one previous occasion, but does not include a person—

(a) whom the solicitor knows, or ought reasonably to know, to be exclusively a client of another solicitor; or

(b) for whom the solicitor has acted only on the instructions of another solicitor.

'practice' means professional practice of a solicitor and includes any area of practice;

'the Secretary' means the Secretary of the Society and includes any person authorised by the Council to act on behalf of the Secretary;

'services' means services provided by a solicitor, and includes any part of such services;

'the Society' means the Law Society of Scotland established under the Act;

'solicitor' means any person enrolled as a solicitor in pursuance of the Act, and includes a firm of solicitors, an incorporated practice and any association of solicitors;

'touting' means a direct approach by or on behalf of a solicitor to a person, who is not an established client, with the intention of soliciting business from that person.

(2) The Interpretation Act 1978 applies to the interpretation of these rules as it applies to the interpretation of an Act of Parliament.

3. The Solicitors (Scotland) Practice Rules 1985 are hereby repealed.

4. Rule 1 of the Solicitors (Scotland) Practice Rules 1964 is hereby repealed.

5. A solicitor shall not apply for or seek instructions for business in such a manner, or do or permit in the carrying on of his practice any such act or thing, as may reasonably be regarded as touting or as calculated to attract business unfairly.

6. A solicitor may, if so requested by or on behalf of any person, provide him with a statement of proposed fees in relation to any services he is willing to provide.

7. Subject to rule 8 hereof, a solicitor shall be entitled to advertise his services in any way he thinks fit, including by means of general circulation of printed material whether or not the persons to whom it is addressed are established clients.

8. An advertisement of or by a solicitor shall not—
(1) claim superiority for the quality of his practice or services over those of, or offered by, other solicitors; or
(2) make reference in relation to any practice to—
(*a*) volume of business or fee income; or
(*b*) the identity of any client except where this is appropriate in any matter which, in the normal course of his practice, the solicitor is instructed by that client to advertise; or
(*c*) any item of business except that which, in the normal course of his practice, he is instructed by a client to advertise; or
(*d*) the outcome of any business carried out for clients; or
(3) compare his fees with those of any other solicitor; or
(4) contain any inaccuracy or misleading statement; or
(5) be by such means or of such a character as may reasonably be regarded as bringing the profession of solicitors into disrepute.

9.—(1) Where an advertisement of or by a solicitor is deemed by the Council to contravene any of these rules, the Council may by written notice duly given to him require the solicitor forthwith, or from such date as the notice may stipulate, to withdraw, terminate or cancel the advertisement, as the case may require, and not to repeat it during the currency of the notice.

(2) A notice given by the Council to a solicitor under paragraph (1) of this rule shall be signed by the Secretary and shall be deemed to have been duly given if it is delivered to him or left at or sent by recorded delivery post to, his last known place of business.

(3) It shall be the duty of a solicitor to obtemper any notice duly given to him under this rule. A solicitor aggrieved by the terms of

any such notice may, within 14 days of the date thereof, make written representations thereanent to the Council, which shall, within two calendar months of the receipt of such representations, either confirm or withdraw said notice; provided that should the Council neither confirm nor withdraw said notice within said period, said notice will be deemed to have been withdrawn at the expiry thereof.

10.—(1) It shall be the duty of a solicitor to ensure that any advertisement of or by him complies with any provision in any practice rules in force for the time being.

(2) An advertisement of or by a solicitor shall, unless the contrary is proved, be deemed to have been issued (in the form in which it was issued) with his authority.

11. The Council shall have power to waive any of the provisions of these rules in any particular case.

12. Breach of any of these rules may be treated as professional misconduct for the purposes of Part IV of the Act (Complaints and Disciplinary Proceedings).

Appendix 5

Code of Conduct for Lawyers in the European Community

Unanimously adopted by the 12 national delegations representing the Bars and the Law Societies of the European Community, at the CCBE Plenary Session, in Strasbourg, on 28 October 1988.

CONTENTS

1.   PREAMBLE

1.1   *The function of the lawyer in society*

In a society founded on respect for the rule of law the lawyer fulfils a special role. His duties do not begin and end with the faithful performance of what he is instructed to do so far as the law permits. A lawyer must serve the interests of justice as well as those whose rights and liberties he is trusted to assert and defend and it is his duty not only to plead his client's cause but to be his adviser.

A lawyer's function therefore lays on him a variety of legal and moral obligations (sometimes appearing to be in conflict with each other) towards:

the client;

the courts and other authorities before whom the lawyer pleads his client's cause or acts on his behalf;

the legal profession in general and each fellow member of it in particular; and

the public for whom the existence of a free and independent profession, bound together by respect for rules made by the profession itself, is an essential means of safeguarding human rights in face of the power of the state and other interests in society.

1.2   *The nature of rules of professional conduct*

1.2.1.   Rules of professional conduct are designed through their willing acceptance by those to whom they apply to ensure the proper performance by the lawyer of a function which is recognised as essential in all civilised societies. The failure of the lawyer to observe these rules must in the last resort result in a disciplinary sanction.

1.2.2   The particular rules of each Bar or Law Society arise from its own traditions. They are adapted to the organisation and sphere of activity of the profession in the Member State concerned and to its judicial and administrative procedures and to its national legislation. It is neither possible nor desirable that they should be taken out of their context nor that an attempt should be made to give general application to rules which are inherently incapable of such application.

The particular rules of each Bar and Law Society nevertheless are based on the same values and in most cases demonstrate a common foundation.

1.3   *The purpose of the code*

1.3.1   The continued integration of the European Community and the increasing frequency of the cross-border activities of lawyers within the Community have made necessary in the public interest the statement of common rules which apply to all lawyers from the Community whatever Bar or Law Society they belong to in relation to their cross-border practice. A particular purpose of the statement of those rules is to mitigate the difficulties which result from the application of 'double deontology' as set out in Article 4 of the E.C. Directive 77/249 of 22nd March 1977.

1.3.2   The organisations representing the legal profession through the CCBE propose that the rules codified in the following articles:

–   be recognised at the present time as the expression of a consensus of all the Bars and Law Societies of the European Community;

–   be adopted as enforceable rules as soon as possible in accordance with national or Community procedures in relation to the cross-border activities of the lawyer in the European Community;

–   be taken into account in all revisions of national rules of deontology or professional practice with a view to their progressive harmonisation.

They further express the wish that the national rules of deontology or professional practice be interpreted and applied whenever possible in a way consistent with the rules of this Code.

After the rules in this Code have been adopted as enforceable rules in relation to his cross-border activities the lawyer will remain bound to observe the rules of the Bar or Law Society to which he belongs to the extent that they are consistent with the rules in this Code.

1.4 *Field of application ratione personae*
The following rules shall apply to lawyers of the European Community as they are defined by the Directive 77/249 of 22nd March 1977.

1.5 *Field of application ratione materiae*
Without prejudice to the pursuit of a progressive harmonisation of rules of deontology or professional practice which apply only internally within a Member State, the following rules shall apply to the cross-border activities of the lawyer within the European Community. Cross-border activities shall mean:
  (a) all professional contacts with lawyers of Member States other than his own; and
  (b) the professional activities of the lawyer in a Member State other than his own, whether or not the lawyer is physically present in that Member State.

1.6 *Definitions*
In these rules:

'Home Member State' means the Member State of the Bar or Law Society to which the lawyer belongs.

'Host Member State' means any other Member State where the lawyer carries on cross-border activities.

'Competent authority' means the professional organisation(s) or authority(ies) of the Member State concerned responsible for the laying down of rules of professional conduct and the administration of discipline of lawyers.

2.   GENERAL PRINCIPLES

2.1   *Independence*

2.1.1   The many duties to which a lawyer is subject require his absolute independence, free from all other influence, especially such as may arise from his personal interests or external pressure. Such independence is as necessary to trust in the process of justice as the impartiality of the judge. A lawyer must therefore avoid any impairment of his independence and be careful not to compromise his professional standards in order to please his client, the court or third parties.

2.1.2   This independence is necessary in non-contentious matters as well as in litigation. Advice given by a lawyer to his client has no value if it is given only to ingratiate himself, to serve his personal interests or in response to outside pressure.

2.2   *Trust and personal integrity*

Relationships of trust can only exist if a lawyer's personal honour, honesty and integrity are beyond doubt. For the lawyer these traditional virtues are professional obligations.

2.3   *Confidentiality*

2.3.1   It is of the essence of a lawyer's function that he should be told by his client things which the client would not tell to others, and that he should be the recipient of other information on a basis of confidence. Without the certainty of confidentiality there cannot be trust. Confidentiality is therefore a primary and fundamental right and duty of the lawyer.

2.3.2   A lawyer shall accordingly respect the confidentiality of all information given to him by his client, or received by him about his client or others in the course of rendering services to his client.

2.3.3   The obligation of confidentiality is not limited in time.

2.3.4   A lawyer shall require his associates and staff and anyone engaged by him in the course of providing professional services to observe the same obligation of confidentiality.

2.4   *Respect for the rules of Other Bars and Law Societies*

Under Community Law (in particular under the Directive 77/249 of 22nd March 1977) a lawyer from another Member State may be bound to comply with the rules of the Bar or Law Society of the host

Member State. Lawyers have a duty to inform themselves as to the rules which will affect them in the performance of any particular activity.

2.5   *Incompatible occupations*

2.5.1   In order to perform his functions with due independence and in a manner which is consistent with his duty to participate in the administration of justice a lawyer is excluded from some occupations.

2.5.2   A lawyer who acts in the representation or the defence of a client in legal proceedings or before any public authorities in a host Member State shall there observe the rules regarding incompatible occupations as they are applied to lawyers of the host Member State.

2.5.3   A lawyer established in a host Member State in which he wishes to participate directly in commercial or other activities not connected with the practice of the law shall respect the rules regarding forbidden or incompatible occupations as they are applied to lawyers of that Member State.

2.6   *Personal publicity*

2.6.1   A lawyer should not advertise or seek personal publicity where this is not permitted.

In other cases a lawyer should only advertise or seek personal publicity to the extent and in the manner permitted by the rules to which he is subject.

2.6.2   Advertising and personal publicity shall be regarded as taking place where it is permitted, if the lawyer concerned shows that it was placed for the purpose of reaching clients or potential clients located where such advertising or personal publicity is permitted and its communication elsewhere is incidental.

2.7   *The client's interests*

Subject to due observance of all rules of law and professional conduct, a lawyer must always act in the best interests of his client and must put those interests before his own interests or those of fellow members of the legal profession.

3.   RELATIONS WITH CLIENTS

3.1   *Acceptance and termination of instructions*

3.1.1   A lawyer shall not handle a case for a party except on his instructions. He may, however, act in a case in which he has been instructed by another lawyer who himself acts for the party or where the case has been assigned to him by a component body.

3.1.2   A lawyer shall advise and represent his client promptly conscientiously and diligently. He shall undertake personal responsibility for the discharge of the instructions given to him. He shall keep his client informed as to the progress of the matter entrusted to him.

3.1.3   A lawyer shall not handle a matter which he knows or ought to know he is not competent to handle, without co-operating with a lawyer who is competent to handle it.

A lawyer shall not accept instructions unless he can discharge those instructions promptly having regard to the pressure of other work.

3.1.4   A lawyer shall not be entitled to exercise his right to withdraw from a case in such a way or in such circumstances that the client may be unable to find other legal assistance in time to prevent prejudice being suffered by the client.

3.2   *Conflict of interest*

3.2.1   A lawyer may not advise, represent or act on behalf of two or more clients in the same matter if there is a conflict, or a significant risk of a conflict, between the interests of those clients.

3.2.2   A lawyer must cease to act for both clients when a conflict of interests arises between those clients and also whenever there is a risk of a breach of confidence or where his independence may be impaired.

3.2.3   A lawyer must also refrain from acting for a new client if there is risk of a breach of confidences entrusted to the lawyer by a former client or if the knowledge which the lawyer possesses of the affairs of the former client would give an undue advantage to the new client.

3.2.4   Where lawyers are practising in association, paragraphs 3.2.1 to 3.2.3 above shall apply to the association and all its members.

3.3 *Pactum de quota litis*

3.3.1 A lawyer shall not be entitled to make a *pactum de quota litis*.

3.3.2 By '*pactum de quota litis*' is meant an agreement between a lawyer and his client entered into prior to the final conclusion of a matter to which the client is a party, by virtue of which the client undertakes to pay the lawyer a share of the result regardless of whether this is represented by a sum of money or by any other benefit achieved by the client upon the conclusion of the matter.

3.3.3 The *pactum de quota litis* does not include an agreement that fees be charged in proportion to the value of a matter handled by the lawyer if this is in accordance with an officially approved fee scale or under the control of the competent authority having jurisdiction over the lawyer.

3.4 *Regulation of fees*

3.4.1 A fee charged by a lawyer shall be fully disclosed to his client and shall be fair and reasonable.

3.4.2 Subject to any proper agreement to the contrary between a lawyer and his client fees charged by a lawyer shall be subject to regulation in accordance with the rules applied to members of the Bar or Law Society to which he belongs. If he belongs to more than one Bar or Law Society the rules applied shall be those with the closest connection to the contract between the lawyer and his client.

3.5 *Payment on account*

If a lawyer requires a payment on account of his fees and/or disbursements such payments should not exceed a reasonable estimate of the fees and probable disbursements involved.

Failing such payment, a lawyer may withdraw from the case or refuse to handle it, but subject always to paragraph 3.1.4 above.

3.6 *Fee sharing with non-lawyers*

3.6.1 Subject as after-mentioned a lawyer may not share his fees with a person who is not a lawyer.

3.6.2 The provisions of 6.1 above shall not preclude a lawyer from paying a fee, commission or other compensation to a deceased lawyer's heirs or to a retired lawyer in respect of taking over the deceased or retired lawyer's practice.

3.7   *Legal aid*
A lawyer shall inform his client of the availability of legal aid where applicable.

3.8   *Client's funds*
3.8.1   When lawyers at any time in the course of their practice come into possession of funds on behalf of their clients or third parties (hereinafter called 'clients' funds') it shall be obligatory:

3.8.1.1   That clients' funds shall always be held in an account in a bank or similar institution subject to supervision of Public Authority and that all clients' funds received by a lawyer should be paid into such an account unless the client explicitly or by implication agrees that the funds should be dealt with otherwise.

3.8.1.2   That any account in which the clients' funds are held in the name of the lawyer should indicate in the title or designation that the funds are held on behalf of the client or clients of the lawyer.

3.8.1.3   That any account or accounts in which clients' funds are held in the name of the lawyer should at all times contain a sum which is not less than the total of the clients' funds held by the lawyer.

3.8.1.4   That all clients' funds should be available for payment to clients on demand or upon such conditions as the client may authorise.

3.8.1.5   That payments made from clients' funds on behalf of a client to any other person including

a) payments made to or for one client from funds held for another client and
b) payment of the lawyer's fees,

be prohibited except to the extent that they are permitted by law or have the express or implied authority of the client for whom the payment is being made.

3.8.1.6   That the lawyer shall maintain full and accurate records, available to each client on request, showing all his dealings with his clients' funds and distinguishing clients' funds from other funds held by him.

3.8.1.7   That the competent authorities in all Member States should have powers to allow them to examine and investigate on a confidential basis the financial records of lawyers' clients' funds to ascertain whether or not the rules which they make are being complied with and to impose sanctions upon lawyers who fail to comply with those rules.

3.8.2 Subject as aftermentioned, and without prejudice to the rules set out in 3.8.1 above, a lawyer who holds clients' funds in the course of carrying on practice in any Member State must comply with the Rules relating to holding and accounting for clients' funds which are applied by the competent authorities of the Home Member State.

3.8.3 A lawyer who carries on practice or provides services in a Host Member State may with the agreement of the competent authorities of the Home and Host Member States concerned comply with the requirements of the Host Member State to the exclusion of the requirements of the Home Member State. In that event he shall take reasonable steps to inform his clients that he complies with the requirements in force in the Host Member State.

3.9 *Professional indemnity insurance*

3.9.1 Lawyers shall be insured at all times against claims based on professional negligence to an extent which is reasonable having regard to the nature and extent of the risks which lawyers incur in practice.

3.9.2.1 Subject as aftermentioned, a lawyer who provides services or carries on practice in a Member State must comply with any Rules relating to his obligation to insure against his professional liability as a lawyer which are in force in his home Member State.

3.9.2.2 A lawyer who is obliged so to insure in his home Member State and who provides services or carries on practice in any Host Member State shall use his best endeavours to obtain insurance cover on the basis required in his home Member State extended to services which he provides or practice which he carries on in a Host Member State.

3.9.2.3 A lawyer who fails to obtain the extended insurance cover referred to in paragraph 3.9.2.2 above or who is not obliged so to insure in his home Member State and who provides services or carries on practice in a Host Member State shall in so far as possible obtain insurance cover against his professional liability as a lawyer whilst acting for clients in that Host Member State on at least an equivalent basis to that required of lawyers in the Host Member State.

3.9.2.4 To the extent that a lawyer is unable to obtain the insurance cover required by the foregoing rules, he shall take reasonable steps to draw that fact to the attention of such of his clients as might be affected in the event of a claim against him.

3.9.2.5 A lawyer who carries on practice or provides services in a Host Member State may with the agreement of the competent authorities of the Home and Host Member States concerned comply with such insurance requirements as are in force in the Host Member State to the exclusion of the insurance requirements of the Home Member State. In this event he shall take reasonable steps to inform his clients that he is insured according to the requirements in force in the Host Member State.

4. RELATIONS WITH THE COURTS

4.1 *Applicable rules of conduct in court*
A lawyer who appears, or takes part in a case, before a court or tribunal in a Member State must comply with the rules of conduct applied before that court or tribunal.

4.2 *Fair conduct of proceedings*
A lawyer must always have due regard for the fair conduct of proceedings. He must not, for example, make contact with the judge without first informing the lawyer acting for the opposing party or submit exhibits, notes or documents to the judge without communicating them in good time to the lawyer on the other side unless such steps are permitted under the relevant rules of procedure.

4.3 *Demeanour in court*
A lawyer shall while maintaining due respect and courtesy towards the court defend the interests of his client honourably and in a way which he considers will be to the client's best advantage within the limits of the law.

4.4 *False or misleading information*
A lawyer shall never knowingly give false or misleading information to the court.

4.5 *Extension to arbitrators etc*
The rules governing a lawyer's relations with the courts apply also to his relations with arbitrators and any other persons exercising judicial or quasi-judicial functions, even on an occasional basis.

5. RELATIONS BETWEEN LAWYERS

5.1 *Corporate spirit of the profession*

5.1.1 The corporate spirit of the profession requires a relationship of trust and co-operation between lawyers for the benefit of their clients and in order to avoid unnecessary litigation. It can never justify setting the interests of the profession against those of justice or of those who seek it.

5.1.2 A lawyer should recognise all other lawyers of Member States as professional colleagues and act fairly and courteously towards them.

5.2 *Co-operation among lawyers of different member states*

5.2.1 It is the duty of a lawyer who is approached by a colleague from another Member State not to accept instructions in a matter which he is not competent to undertake. He should be prepared to help his colleague to obtain the information necessary to enable him to instruct a lawyer who is capable of providing the service asked for.

5.2.2 Where a lawyer of a Member State co-operates with a lawyer from another Member State, both have a general duty to take into account the differences which may exist between their respective legal systems and the professional organisations competences and obligations of lawyers in the Member States concerned.

5.3 *Correspondence between lawyers*

5.3.1 If a lawyer sending a communication to a lawyer in another Member State wishes it to remain confidential or without prejudice he should clearly express this intention when communicating the document.

5.3.2 If the recipient of the communication is unable to ensure its status as confidential or without prejudice he should return it to the sender without revealing the contents to others.

5.4   *Referral fees*

5.4.1   A lawyer may not demand or accept from another lawyer or any other person a fee, commission or any other compensation for referring or recommending a client.

5.4.2   A lawyer may not pay anyone a fee, commission or any other compensation as a consideration for referring a client to himself.

5.5   *Communication with opposing parties*

A lawyer shall not communicate about a particular case or matter directly with any person whom he knows to be represented or advised in the case or matter by another lawyer, without the consent of that other lawyer (and shall keep the other lawyer informed of any such communications).

5.6   *Change of lawyer*

5.6.1   A lawyer who is instructed to represent a client in substitution for another lawyer in relation to a particular matter should inform that other lawyer and, subject to 5.6.2 below, should not begin to act until he has ascertained that arrangements have been made for the settlement of the other lawyer's fees and disbursements. This duty does not, however, make the new lawyer personally responsible for the former lawyer's fees and disbursements.

5.6.2   If urgent steps have to be taken in the interests of the client before the conditions in 5.6.1 above can be complied with, the lawyer may take such steps provided he informs the other lawyer immediately.

5.7   *Responsibility for fees*

In professional relations between members of Bars of different Member States, where a lawyer does not confine himself to recommending another lawyer or introducing him to the client but himself entrusts a correspondent with a particular matter or seeks his advice, he is personally bound, even if the client is insolvent, to pay the fees, costs and outlays which are due to the foreign correspondent. The lawyers concerned may, however, at the outset of the relationship between them make special arrangements on this matter. Further, the instructing lawyer may at any time limit his personal responsibility to the amount of the fees, costs and outlays incurred before intimation to the foreign lawyer of his disclaimer of responsibility for the future.

5.8   *Training young lawyers*

In order to improve trust and co-operation amongst lawyers of different Member States for the clients' benefit there is a need to encourage a better knowledge of the laws and procedures in different Member States. Therefore when considering the need for the profession to give good training to young lawyers, lawyers should take into account the need to give training to young lawyers from other Member States.

5.9   *Disputes amongst lawyers in different Member States*

5.9.1   If a lawyer considers that a colleague in another Member State has acted in breach of a rule of professional conduct he shall draw the matter to the attention of his colleague.

5.9.2   If any personal dispute of a professional nature arises amongst lawyers in different Member States they should if possible first try to settle it in a friendly way.

5.9.3   A lawyer shall not commence any form of proceedings against a colleague in another Member State on matters referred to in 5.9.1 or 5.9.2 above without first informing the Bars or Law Societies to which they both belong for the purpose of allowing both Bars or Law Societies concerned an opportunity to assist in reaching a settlement.

Appendix 6

Solicitors (Scotland) Practice Rules 1986

1. (1) These Rules may be cited as the Solicitors (Scotland) Practice Rules 1986.

(2) These Rules shall come into operation with respect to transactions commenced on or after 1st January, 1987.

2. (1) In these Rules, unless the context otherwise requires:

'the Act' means the Solicitors (Scotland) Act 1980;

'client' includes prospective client;

'Council' means the Council of the Society;

'established client' means a person for whom a solicitor or his firm has acted on at least one previous occasion;

'employed solicitor' means a solicitor employed by his employer for the purpose, wholly or partly, of offering legal services to the public whether or not for a fee;

'firm' includes any office at which that firm carries on practice and any firm in which that firm has a direct interest through one or more of its partners, or members;

'the Society' means the Law Society of Scotland established under the Act;

'solicitor' means a solicitor holding a practising certificate under the Act, or an incorporated practice;

'transaction' includes a contract and any negotiations leading thereto.

(2) The Interpretation Act 1978 applies to the interpretation of these Rules as it applies to the interpretation of an Act of Parliament.

3. A solicitor shall not act for two or more parties whose interests conflict.

4. Without prejudice to the generality of Rule 3 hereof an employed solicitor whose only or principal employer is one of the parties to a transaction shall not act for any other party to that transaction; provided always that such solicitor may, where no dispute arises or appears likely to arise between the parties to that transaction, act for more than one party thereto, if and only if:

(a) the parties are associated companies, public authorities, public bodies, or Government Departments or Agencies;

(b) the parties are connected one with the other within the meaning of section 533 Income and Corporation Taxes Act 1970.

5. (1) Without prejudice to the generality of Rule 3 hereof, a solicitor, or two or more solicitors practising either as principal or employee in the same firm or in the employment of the same employer, shall not at any stage, act for both seller and purchaser in the sale or purchase or conveyance of heritable property, or for both landlord and tenant, or assignor and assignee in a lease of heritable property for value or for lender and borrower in a loan to be secured over heritable property; provided, however, that where no dispute arises or might reasonably be expected to arise between the parties and that, other than in the case of exception (a) hereto, the seller or landlord of residential property is not a builder or developer, this Rule shall not apply if:

(a) the parties are associated companies, public authorities, public bodies, or Government Departments or Agencies;

(b) the parties are connected one with the other within the meaning of section 533 Income and Corporation Taxes Act 1970;

(c) the parties are related by blood, adoption or marriage, one to the other, or the purchaser, tenant, assignee or borrower is so related to an established client; or

(d) both parties are established clients or the prospective purchaser, tenant, assignee or borrower is an established client; or

(e) there is no other solicitor in the vicinity whom the client could reasonably be expected to consult; or

(f) in the case of a loan to be secured over heritable property, the terms of the loan have been agreed between the parties before the solicitor has been instructed to act for the lender, and the granting of the security is only to give effect to such agreement.

(2) In all cases falling within exceptions (c), (d) and (e) both parties shall be advised by the solicitor at the earliest practicable opportunity that the solicitor, or his firm, has been requested to act for both parties, and that if a dispute arises, they or one of them will require to consult an independent solicitor or solicitors, which advice shall be confirmed by the solicitor in writing as soon as may be practicable thereafter.

6. A solicitor shall unless the contrary be proved be presumed for the purposes of Rules 4 and 5 thereof to be acting for a party for whom he prepares an offer whether complete or not, in connection with a transaction of any kind specified in these Rules, for execution by that party.

7. A solicitor acting on behalf of a party or prospective party to a transaction of any kind specified in Rule 5 hereof shall not issue any deed, writ, missive or other document requiring the signature of another party or prospective party to him without informing that party in writing that:

(a) such signature may have certain legal consequences, and

(b) he should seek independent legal advice before signature.

8. Where a solicitor, or two or more solicitors practising as principal or employee in the same firm or in the employment of the same employer, knowingly intends or intend to act on behalf of two or more prospective purchasers or tenants (other than prospective joint purchasers or tenants) of heritable property (in this Rule referred to as 'the clients'), the clients shall be informed of such intention, and a single solicitor shall not, where he has given any advice to one of the clients with respect to the price or rent to be offered, or with respect to any other material condition of the prospective bargain, give advice to another of the clients in respect of such matters.

9. The Council shall have power to waive any of the provisions of these Rules in any particular circumstances or case.

10. Breach of any of these Rules may be treated as professional misconduct for the purposes of Part IV of the Act (Complaints and Disciplinary Proceedings).

Appendix 7

Code of Conduct for Scottish Solicitors

Issued by the Law Society of Scotland for guidance in assessing whether or not a solicitor's conduct meets the standard required of a member of the profession.

Contents

Introduction

In common with lawyers in most parts of the world, solicitors in Scotland have always been expected, by the general public and by their professional colleagues and others, to observe certain standards of professional conduct. The standards are required in order to establish the essential relationship of trust between lawyer and client, between lawyer and court, and between lawyer and other members of the legal profession.

181

All solicitors in Scotland require to be members of the Law Society of Scotland and for many years specific practice rules have been promulgated by the Society as a self-regulatory organisation for solicitors. Some of these rules have been included in Acts of Parliament and the Society's authority for promulgating additional practice rules comes from Parliament itself and the rules are subject to the consent of the Lord President of the Court of Session. These rules are binding upon solicitors. They stem from and have the force of statutory authority.

The law of Scotland was and is founded upon principles which have the same validity and authority as Acts of Parliament. In the same way, in addition to the written rules governing solicitors in Scotland, there are other commonly accepted standards of conduct which solicitors are expected to meet.

The CCBE (Conseil des Barreaux de la Communaute Europeenne), comprising representatives of all the governing bodies of lawyers in the European Community, adopted in 1988 a Code of Conduct for lawyers within the community which governs conduct of lawyers in relation to activities crossing over from one country to another.

In addition, the CCBE Code is to be taken into account in all revisions of national rules with a view to the progressive harmonisation of codes and regulations governing lawyers within the European Community.

All the standards of professional conduct, whether contained in Acts of Parliament or in practice rules (written or unwritten) which are binding upon solicitors in Scotland are based upon certain values and principles which form the foundation of the profession and reflect the legal, moral and professional obligations of the solicitor to:

the clients;

the courts and other authorities before whom a lawyer pleads his client's cause or acts on his behalf;

the public; and

the legal profession in general and each fellow member of it in particular.

Should any solicitor transgress any of these rules, then such transgression may give rise to disciplinary proceedings and amount to professional misconduct or some lesser finding.

The following Code contains a statement of the basic values and principles which form the foundation of the solicitor profession. It is not intended to be an exhaustive list of all the detailed practice rules and detailed obligations of solicitors, but it is the foundation for those rules and may be referred to for guidance in assessing whether or not a solicitor's conduct meets the standard required of a member of the profession.

Preamble

I. The function of the lawyer in society

In a society founded on respect for the rule of law lawyers fulfil a special role. Their duties do not begin and end with the faithful performance of what they are instructed to do so far as the law permits. Lawyers must serve the interests of justice as well as those whose rights and liberties they are trusted to assert and defend and it is their duty not only to plead their clients' cause but also to be their adviser.

The function of lawyers therefore imposes on them a variety of legal and moral obligations (sometimes appearing to be in conflict with each other) towards:—

(a) the clients;
(b) the courts and other authorities before whom the lawyers plead their clients' cause or act on their behalf;
(c) the public for whom the existence of a free and independent profession, bound together by respect for rules made by the profession itself, is an essential means of safeguarding human rights in face of the power of the state and other interests in society.
(d) the legal profession in general and each fellow member of it in particular.

II. The nature of rules of professional conduct

Rules of professional conduct are designed to ensure the proper performance by the lawyer of a function which is recognised as essential in all civilised societies. The failure of the lawyer to observe these rules must in the last resort result in a disciplinary sanction. The willing acceptance of those rules and of the need for disciplinary sanction ensures the highest possible standards.

The particular rules of all the Bar Associations and Law Societies in the European Community are based on identical values and in most cases demonstrate a common foundation which is also reflected in Bar Associations and Law Societies throughout the world.

The Code

1. Independence

Independence is essential to the function of solicitors in their relationships with all parties and it is the duty of all solicitors that they do not allow their independence to be impaired irrespective of whether or not the matter in which they are acting involves litigation.

Independence means that solicitors must not allow themselves to be restricted in their actings on behalf of or in giving advice to their clients, nor must they allow themselves to be influenced by motives inconsistent with the principles of this Code. For example, solicitors must not compromise their professional standards in order to promote their own interests or the interests of parties other than their clients. Advice must not be given simply to ingratiate solicitors with their clients, courts or third parties. Non-independent advice may be worse than useless in that it may actively encourage someone to undertake a course of action which is not in his or her best interests.

When representing clients in court solicitors appear as agents and speak for their clients, but this does not mean that they are permitted to put forward statements or arguments which they know to be untruthful or misleading. Similarly, in relation to other services solicitors although acting as agents, must remain independent for their advice and actings to be of value.

2. The interests of the client

Solicitors must always act in the best interests of their clients subject to preserving their independence as solicitors and to the due observance of the law, professional practice rules and the principles of good professional conduct. Solicitors must not permit their own personal interests or those of the legal profession in general to influence their actings on behalf of clients; further, their actings must be free of all political considerations.

Solicitors in advising clients must not allow their advice to be influenced by the fact that a particular course of action would result in the solicitor being able to charge a higher fee; solicitors are not permitted to 'buy' or pay for business introductions, although commission may be paid to a fellow lawyer.

Solicitors should not allow themselves to be persuaded by clients to pursue matters or courses of action which the solicitors consider not to be in the clients' interests. It may be appropriate for solicitors to refuse to act where clients are not prepared to follow the advice given.

Where solicitors are consulted about matters in which they have a personal or a financial interest the position should be made clear to the clients and where appropriate solicitors should insist that the clients consult other solicitors. For example, neither a solicitor, nor a partner of that solicitor, is generally permitted to prepare a will for a client where the solicitor is to receive a significant legacy or share of the estate.

Solicitors are the agents of their clients and as such are not permitted to conceal any profit deriving from their actings for clients and must make known to their clients the source of any commission so arising.

3. Conflict

Solicitors (including firms of solicitors) shall not act for two or more clients in matters where there is a conflict of interest between the clients or for any client where there is a conflict between the interest of the client and that of the solicitor or the solicitor's firm.

In considering whether or not to accept instructions from more than one party and where there is potential for a conflict arising at a later date, solicitors must have regard to any possible risk of breaches of confidentiality and impairment of independence. If, having decided to proceed, a conflict should later arise solicitors must not continue to act for all the parties and in most cases they will require to withdraw from acting for all of the parties. There may, however, be certain circumstances which would result in a significant disadvantage to one party were the solicitor not to continue to act for that party and there is no danger of any breach of confidentiality in relation to the other party. In these very special cases, the solicitor may continue to act for one party.

Solicitors must accept instructions only from clients or recognised agents authorised to give instructions on behalf of the clients; for example, persons authorised by a power of attorney or another lawyer. Where a solicitor is requested to act for more than one party in respect of the same matter, the solicitor must be reasonably satisfied that there is no apparent conflict among the interests of all the parties and that each party is indeed authorising the solicitor to act.

4. Confidentiality

The observance of client confidentiality is a fundamental duty of solicitors.

This duty applies not only to the solicitors but also to their partners and staff, and the obligation is not terminated by the passage of time. This principle is so important that it is recognised by the courts as being esssential to the administration of justice and to the relationship of trust which must exist between solicitor and client. Only in special circumstances may a court require a solicitor to break the obligation of confidentiality.

5. Provision of a professional service

Solicitors must provide adequate professional services.

Solicitors are under a professional obligation to provide adequate professional services to their clients. An adequate professional service requires the legal knowledge, skill, thoroughness and preparation necessary to the matter in hand. Solicitors should not accept instructions unless they can adequately discharge these. This means that as well as being liable for damages assessable by a court of law for any act of negligence in dealing with a client's affairs, a solicitor may face disciplinary action by the Law Society in respect of a service to a client which is held to be an inadequate professional service.

(a) Solicitors must act on the basis of their clients' proper instructions or on the instructions of another solicitor who acts for the client..

Solicitors act as the agents of the clients and must have the authority of the clients for their actions.

A client may withdraw authority at any time by giving due notification to the solicitor. However, such withdrawal cannot act retrospectively.

Solicitors require to discuss with and advise their clients on the objectives of the work carried out on behalf of the clients and the means by which the objectives are to be pursued. Acceptance of instructions from clients does not constitute an endorsement or approval of the clients' political, social or moral views, activities or motivations. With the agreement of the client a solicitor may restrict the objectives and the steps to be taken consistent with the provision of an adequate professional service. A solicitor may not accept an improper instruction; for example, to assist a client in a matter which the solicitor knows to be criminal or fraudulent, but a solicitor may advise on the legal consequences of any proposed course of conduct or assist a client in determining the validity, scope or application of the law.

Solicitors are free to refuse to undertake instructions, but once acting should withdraw from a case or transaction only for good cause and where possible in such a manner that the clients' interests are not adversely affected. This obligation will not, however, prevent solicitors from exercising their rights at law to recover their justified fees and outlays incurred on behalf of their clients.

(b) A solicitor shall act only in those matters where the solicitor is competent to do so.

Where a solicitor considers that the service to a client would be inadequate owing to the solicitor's lack of knowledge or experience it would be improper for the solicitor to accept instructions and agree to act.

(c) Solicitors shall accept instructions only where the matter can be carried out with due expedition and solicitors shall maintain appropriate systems in order to ensure that the matter is dealt with effectively.

Where a solicitor considers, for example, that the service to a client would be inadequate, owing to pressure of work or the like so that the matter would not be dealt with within a reasonable period of time, it would be improper for the solicitor to accept instructions and agree to act.

(d) Solicitors are required to exercise the level of skill appropriate to the matter.

In deciding whether or not to accept instructions from a client, and in the carrying out of those instructions, a solicitor must have regard to the nature and complexity of the matter in hand and apply to the work the appropriate level of professional skills.

(e) Solicitors shall communicate effectively with their clients and others.

Solicitors are required to try to ensure that their communications with their clients and others on behalf of their clients are effective. This includes providing clients with relevant information regarding the matter in hand and the actions taken on their behalf. Solicitors should advise their clients of any significant development in relation to their case or transaction and explain matters to the extent reasonably necessary to permit informed decisions by clients regarding the instructions which require to be given by them. Information should be clear and comprehensive and where necessary or appropriate confirmed in writing.

The duty to communicate effectively extends to include the obligation on solicitors to account to their clients in respect of all relevant monies passing through the solicitor's hands.

(f) Solicitors shall not act, nor shall they cease to act for clients summarily or without just cause, in a manner which would prejudice the course of justice.

Where the matter in issue involves the courts or otherwise involves the administration of justice, a solicitor must have regard to the course of justice in considering whether or not to cease acting on behalf of a client. The solicitor may not simply and suddenly decide that it would no longer be appropriate to act for the client and in most cases the solicitor will require to seek the agreement of the court to the withdrawal of the solicitor's services.

(g) Solicitors shall comply with the specific rules issued from time to time by the Law Society of Scotland.

Subject to the consent of the Lord President of the Court of Session the Law Society is empowered to issue specific practice rules regarding the conduct of solicitors and other matters affecting the affairs of clients. All solicitors must comply with these rules. A list of the titles of such rules currently in force is annexed to this code.

6. Professional fees

The fees charged by solicitors shall be fair and reasonable in all the circumstances.

Factors to be considered in relation to the reasonableness of the fee include:—

(a) the importance of the matter to the client;
(b) the amount of value of any money, property or transaction involved;
(c) the complexity of the matter or the difficulty or novelty of the question raised;
(d) the skill, labour, specialised knowledge and responsibility involved on the part of the solicitor;
(e) the time expended;
(f) the length, number and importance of any documents or other papers prepared or perused; and
(g) the place where and the circumstances in which the services or any part thereof are rendered and the degree of urgency involved.

7. Trust and personal integrity

Solicitors must act honestly at all times and in such a way as to put their personal integrity beyond question.

Solicitors' actions and personal behaviour must be consistent with the need for mutual trust and confidence among clients, the courts, the public and fellow lawyers. For example, solicitors must observe the Accounts Rules which govern the manner in which clients' funds may be held by solicitors and which are designed to ensure that clients' monies are safeguarded. Solicitors who are dishonest in a matter not directly affecting their clients are nonetheless guilty of professional misconduct.

8. Relations with the courts

Solicitors must never knowingly give false or misleading information to court and must maintain due respect and courtesy towards the court while honourably pursuing the interests of their clients.

For example, it would be improper for a solicitor to put forward on behalf of a client a statement of events or a legal argument which the solicitor knew to be false or misleading. Accordingly, if a client requests a solicitor to put forward a false story the solicitor must refuse to do so.

In the course of investigation a solicitor must not do or say anything which could affect evidence or induce a witness, a party to an action, or an accused person to do otherwise than give in evidence a truthful and honest statement of that person's recollections.

9. Relations between lawyers

Solicitors shall not knowingly mislead colleagues or where they have given their word go back on it.

A solicitor must act with fellow solicitors in a manner consistent with persons having mutual trust and confidence in each other.

It is in the public interest and for the benefit of clients and the administration of justice that there be a corporate professional spirit based upon relationships of trust and co-operation between solicitors. For example, the settlement of property transactions in Scotland is facilitated by the underlying trust between solicitors. A specific example of this is the payment of the price by a cheque drawn by the purchaser's solicitor on a joint stock bank in favour of the seller's solicitor. Were the purchaser's solicitor to instruct the bank to stop payment of the cheque such action could amount to professional misconduct.

It is not permissible for a solicitor to communicate about any item of business with a person whom the solicitor knows to be represented by another solicitor. A solicitor in such circumstances must always communicate with the solicitor acting for that person and not go behind the solicitor's back.

The rules governing the advertising of solicitors' services take into account the need to maintain mutual trust and confidence, while permitting solicitors to market their services effectively and to compete with one another.

10. Civil professionalism

Solicitors have a duty not only to act as guardians of national liberties, but also to seek improvements in the law and the legal system.

It is the striving by solicitors for improvement both in general terms and in relation to the individual needs of a particular client that prevents the law and legal services 'from degenerating into a trade or mere mechanical act' (Lord Cooper, Selected Papers, Edinburgh 1957, p. 77). Many solicitors fulfil this obligation through working on the many Committees of the Law Society of Scotland, including those not only commenting and advising on proposed legislative changes and areas of law reform but also recommending and promoting new ideas for reform. Others are involved at the highest level with other reforming bodies and many seek public appointment, both locally and at a national level.

This duty extends beyond the issues of freedom and liberty, through the entire system of law, to the day-to-day legal services provided by solicitors.

Appendix

Practice Rules of the Law Society of Scotland *currently in force*

Solicitors (Scotland) Practice Rules 1964

Solicitors (Scotland) Practice Rules 1975

Admission as Solicitor (Scotland) Regulations 1976

Solicitors (Scotland) Practice Rules 1981

Scottish Solicitors Guarantee Fund Rules 1981

Admission as Solicitor (Scotland) Regulations 1986

Solicitors (Scotland) Practice Rules 1986

Solicitors (Scotland) (Advertising) Practice Rules 1987

Solicitors (Scotland) (Incorporated Practices) Practice Rules 1987

Solicitors (Scotland) (Conduct of Investment Business) Practice Rules 1988

Solicitors (Scotland) Compliance Certificate Rules 1988

Solicitors (Scotland) Practising Certificate Rules 1988

Solicitors (Scotland) Professional Indemnity Insurance Rules 1988

Solicitors (Scotland) Accounts Rules 1989

Solicitors (Scotland) Accountant's Certificate Rules 1989

Solicitors (Scotland) (Attendance at Courses on Practice Management) Practice Rules 1989

Solicitors (Scotland) (Associates, Consultants and Employees) Practice Rules 1989

Solicitors (Scotland) (Cross Border Code of Conduct) Practice Rules 1989

Solicitors (Scotland) (Conduct of Investment Business) Practice Rules 1989